The Money book,

chains to change

By Jm Alexander

The Digital Trap

Jm Alexander

Published by Yellaboy Productions, 2025.

THE DIGITAL TRAP

First edition. June 21, 2025.

ISBN: 979-8231117543

Written by Jm Alexander.

Table of Contents

Dedication

To Ashton and Jakob—

My grown children, my forever blessings.

I wasn't always there when you needed me most,

but not a day has passed that you haven't been on my mind and in my heart.

Time and distance never dimmed my love—

it only made it louder in silence.

This is for you,

a small offering for all the moments I missed.

I love you more than words have ever said.

Foreword:

Yo... welcome to the game you never signed up for.They didn't hand you a rulebook when you were born, did they? Just smacked you on the ass, gave you a number, and told you to chase paper like it's salvation. But here's the twist nobody tells you: the game is rigged. The house always wins. And the ones printing the money? They already bought the board, the dice, the dealer, and the damn rulebook.This ain't just a book. This is a flashlight in a pitch-black vault. A siren blaring through the silence of propaganda. This is The Money Book, and you're not supposed to be reading it.

Because the more you know about how money really works, the more you'll question the whole damn thing.

Why are a handful of men worth more than entire countries? Why is someone working 40, 60, 80 hours a week still drowning in debt while billionaires dodge taxes like it's a sport? Why are we told to budget better when the Fed can print infinite cash and hand it to corporations like candy?

This book is your red pill. I'm not here to sell you hope. I'm here to sell you the truth. If that's too raw for you, put it down now. If you're ready to get uncomfortable, let's ride.

Chapter 1: Trillionaire Season – The New Pharaohs of Finance

"There will be five trillionaires within the next decade."

Let that marinate for a second.

Have you ever tried to imagine a trillion dollars? Not a million. Not a billion. A trillion.It's a number so big it breaks the human brain. You could buy every single NFL, NBA, MLB, and NHL team three times over... and still have billions left to start your own league. You could snatch up GM, Ford, KFC, Pizza Hut, Taco Bell, and still have enough leftovers to make it rain on a small nation. You could bankroll political campaigns, rewrite laws, even sponsor a war—and still sleep with billions in the bank.Now ask yourself this: If someone had that much money... you think they wouldn't own presidents?You think the man who can buy a country wouldn't also buy its laws?That's the new empire, fam. These trillionaire titans ain't rich—they're kings without crowns, emperor's inAirPods

.

Let's zoom in. Look at Zuck.As of now, Mark Zuckerberg is sitting on $236 billion. That's not rich. That's galactic. A $5 coffee for him is like you spending one-thousandth of a penny. Buying a $1 million house for him? That's a quarter. Filling up a gas tank? A penny.

Here's the math that'll make your stomach flip: if Zuck gave away a million dollars every single day, it would take him 646 years to go broke. That's 7 lifetimes of generosity—and he still wouldn't touch poverty.The game is wild.You work 20 years to retire with a few hundred grand, praying your body holds up. He earns your entire life's salary while brushing his teeth. And it's not just Zuck. Elon. Bezos. The Walton family. BlackRock. Vanguard. These entities aren't just wealthy. They own the wealth.Let's break it down.

The Four Americas

We got $164 trillion in wealth in the U.S. Sounds impressive, right? Except it ain't spread evenly.Top 1% (3.3M people): $50 trillion.Next 9% (30M people): $60 trillion.

Next 40% (133M people): $50 trillion.

Bottom 50% (175M people): $4 trillion.

Read that again.Half the country fights over $4 trillion while the top 10% sits on $110 trillion. That's not inequality—that's economic apartheid.And here's where it gets sick: in 1980, adjusted for inflation, America's wealth was $30 trillion. Today it's $164 trillion. But the bottom 50% only saw their share grow by $2 trillion, while the top exploded by over $130 trillion.

That's not trickle-down economics. That's a damn heist.And worse? There's 60 million more people in the bottom 50% today, meaning that $4 trillion gets split thinner than a communion wafer.

We're not just being left behind—we're being robbed in slow motion.

The Fed and the Illusion of Wealth

Have you ever wondered how the rich got richer during a pandemic?It's because the Federal Reserve printed trillions out of thin air and handed it straight to the top through asset inflation. Wall Street got a sugar rush. Main Street got evicted.

The Fed isn't your friend. They're the bouncer at the door of wealth, and only billionaires are on the list. Infinite money exists—but only if you're already rich. They gave trillions to BlackRock, to State Street, to the same wolves who caused the last crash.Your rent went up. Their portfolio doubled.

Your job got outsourced. Their stocks hit record highs.This ain't capitalism. This is corporate feudalism. And the Fed is the printing press for the kings.JFK saw it. That's why he tried to issue silver certificates and challenge the central banking cartel. Then... bang. Lights out. But that's another chapter.Wages Ain't WealthYou ever hear that line: "Just work hard, save your money, and invest."

Cute. But let me show you why it's a fantasy.Let's say you make $160k a year. That's the top 1% income in the UK. You save half, every year, starting from the moment you were born (no diapers, no expenses). It'd still take you 76 years to crack the bottom edge of 1% wealth.

Because income is rented power.

Wealth is inherited control.Your salary makes you feel rich while you build someone else's empire. And if you ever get too bold—like organizing, striking, protesting—they'll just cut the checkbook and replace you with AI, or someone hungrier from a poorer country.

—-

They Say We're Broke. We're Being Robbed Governments always crying broke, right?"No money for food stamps." "No budget for disability checks." "No funding for public schools." Meanwhile, the top 5 families in the UK hold more wealth than 13 million people combined. The top 50 families outpace half the entire country. But yeah—let's take away £40 a week from someone with MS.This isn't a crisis.

It's a robbery in broad daylight. A heist in a three-piece suit with a Harvard degree. They've convinced us the getaway driver is the poor, the sick, the immigrants, the homeless. While the real crooks fly private and file taxes in Bermuda.

Conclusion: Know the Game, Play It Loud

Capitalism in 2025 is not about innovation. It's not about fairness. It's about extraction. You're the resource. Your labor, your time, your data, your energy. They monetize your attention, your desperation, your hope.But here's the truth they don't want you to realize: you are the engine.

No Amazon driver, no package. No teacher, no learning. No janitor, no hospital. No farmer, no food. No coder, no app. No labor, no wealth.

When we stop pretending they're gods, we start remembering our power. We stop waiting for a savior and start becoming the storm.

—-

Chapter 2: Digital Chains & Invisible Hands

The future came wearing a hoodie, whispering promises of ease and access. With every swipe, tap, and scan, we stepped deeper into a system designed not to empower—but to imprison. Convenience, they said. Security. Progress. But behind every cashless transaction lies a chain—silent, digital, invisible.Cash was king. Then it got dethroned.Now? Algorithms rule.We didn't notice the empire fall. We were too busy chasing likes, upgrades, and next-day delivery. What replaced the king wasn't a better ruler. It was a godless ghost—a decentralized network of control, owned by no one, operated by everyone, manipulated by the few. And we? Just willing servants on a smart leash.

The Death of Tangibility

Remember the feel of a crisp twenty? The ragged edge of an old five? That smell of paper money? That was power. That was independence. Anonymous. Untraceable. Yours.Then came Venmo. Then came CashApp. Then Zelle. Then Apple Pay. Tap here. Blink there. Soon came Central Bank Digital Currencies (CBDCs), and boom—money became code. Ones and zeroes. Data wrapped in firewalls and falsehoods. Once they digitized the dollar, they digitized your life.

No cash? No freedom.

They called it "financial inclusion." But inclusion ain't freedom. Inclusion just means you're inside—inside the prison.

The Rise of CBDCs: Control in Your Pocket

The central banks said, "We'll make it easier for the unbanked." Translation: We'll get every soul onto the grid. And once you're on it, you can't leave.

CBDCs ain't just digital dollars. They're programmable. Spend limits. Expiration dates. Purchase restrictions. Don't want you buying red meat? Blocked. Speaking against the regime? Frozen. Missed your carbon credit quota? Denied.This isn't some Orwellian fantasy. It's already happening.

China's digital yuan has geolocation tracking and smart contracts that expire. Nigeria launched its eNaira. The European Central Bank's digital euro is almost ready. America? Quietly laying the groundwork, calling it "FedNow."

Cashless means they control when, where, and how you live.

The invisible hands are real—and they type.Surveillance Capitalism: You Are the ProductMoney ain't just green paper no more. It's metadata. Spending patterns. Behavioral footprints. Your coffee habit is worth more than your credit score. That's why Big Tech wants in.

Google Pay. Apple Wallet. Amazon One (pay with your palm, literally). Facebook's abandoned Libra coin? Just the first shot in a silent war for your identity.

See, when you walk into a store and use your card, it's not a purchase. It's a data upload. They know what you buy, when you buy, how often, and how emotional you were when you clicked "confirm."

This ain't just targeted ads. This is predictive control. You ever wonder how the algorithm knows you're sad before you do? That's not magic—it's math, weaponized.

Financial Social Credit Scores Are Coming

They tested it in China. Now the blueprint's global.Imagine this: You tweet a hot take against the wrong politician. Suddenly, your bank app glitches. Can't book a flight. Uber won't work. Your rent payment "fails." Not a bug—by design.

Western governments won't call it a social credit system. They'll brand it as ESG compliance, digital ID verification, and AI fraud protection.

But it's all the same net. Different branding. Same trap.

Debanked. De-platformed. De-personed.

The worst part? You'll have no appeal. The algorithm already judged you. No court. No jury. Just code.NFTs, Crypto, and the Great Illusion of FreedomNow I hear some of y'all shouting: "What about Bitcoin?! What about crypto? We got freedom coins!"Slow down.Crypto had potential. Still does. But just like hip-hop, it got commercialized. Colonized. Institutionalized.Bitcoin started as a rebellion. Now BlackRock's got ETFs. JPMorgan running Ethereum nodes. Your crypto wallets? KYC'd. Your privacy coins? Delisted.

And NFTs? That was just Silicon Valley's version of Beanie Babies, wrapped in hype and sold with a sprinkle of "ownership" sauce.Don't get it twisted. Blockchain tech is powerful. Decentralization is necessary. But until we own the rails, not just ride them, we still slaves—just with cooler chains.Digital Wallets Are Trojan Horses

They told you to get that mobile wallet for security. Truth is, it's a Trojan horse.

Apple Pay, Google Pay, and even government digital IDs—all they need is your thumbprint, your face scan, and your consent. One day, your bank will ask for facial verification. Then voice. Then behavior analysis. All in the name of "protection."Soon, your wallet won't just know your balance. It'll know your mood, your blood pressure, your biometric rhythm. All synced with your smart fridge, your wearable, your car.

It won't ask, "Can you afford it?"

It'll ask, "Should you be allowed to?"

The End of Ownership

They said we're entering the "access economy." Sounded good. But access ain't ownership.Spotify gave us access to music. Now you own none. Netflix gave us access to movies. No DVDs. Kindle gave us eBooks. They can delete them at will.

Your money? Soon the same.

CBDCs can disappear overnight. Crypto can be frozen. Stocks turned to code, brokered by apps that can rug-pull your portfolio if you misbehave.

You won't own money.You'll rent it.

And they'll charge you for late fees in carbon.The Psychological Warfare of Financial DependencyThe goal isn't just control. It's submission.Financial instability breeds obedience. When rent's due, fridge is empty, and job's at risk, you'll do anything. Say anything. Believe anything.

They don't need guns when they get your wallet.

Universal Basic Income? Sounded sweet. But what if your UBI comes with fine print? Agree to these terms. Stay within this behavior score. Take this shot. Post this flag. Silence that opinion.Financial fear becomes self-censorship.

We won't need thought police. We'll police ourselves.From Pyramids to Pixels: The New PlantationThis ain't capitalism. This is neo-feudalism, digitized.You got:Tech pharaohs building pyramids out of code.

Data slaves mining likes, clicks, and compliance.Financial priests in central banks printing salvation—or damnation.

And the rest of us? Harvested.

The plantation's wireless now. But the chains still click.Solutions or Survival Tactics?I won't lie to you. Ain't no simple answer. But here's where we start:

. Cash is resistance. Keep it alive. Use it when you can. Teach your kids its value.

Real assets matter. Land. Gold. Food. Skills. The physical world can't be hacked.Decentralized platforms. Support open-source tech. Learn peer-to-peer systems. Run your own node.

Community over cloud. Build with people you can touch. Organize offline. Trust faces, not interfaces.Digital hygiene. Limit your exposure. Burn the algorithm. Don't trade privacy for dopamine.And most of all—Stay awake.This isn't just about dollars. It's about destiny. Your financial life is spiritual warfare now. They want your soul behind a paywall.

Final Thought: Money or Mastery?

We ain't chasing money no more. We're chasing mastery. Over systems. Over self. Over fear.

They built a system so slick, so seductive, we thought it was freedom. But every convenience has a cost. Every app is a trap. Every update, a deeper lock.This ain't paranoia. This is a prophecy.

You were warned.So ask yourself: when they turn off the tap, lock the code, freeze the funds...Will you still eat?Will you still breathe free?Or will you kneel, digitized and dehumanized, begging for a top-up?

Choose now.Because the future's already loading.

—-

—-

Chapter 3: "Burn the Blueprint, Build Your Own"

They gave us a blueprint. Neatly folded. Glossy. Came with slogans.Go to school."Get a job.""Save in a 401k.""Buy a house." "Retire at 65."But here's the reality: that blueprint was a damn trap.A choke collar made of debt, dependency, and distraction. A hamster wheel sold as a highway. A paycheck laced with poison. And every generation handed it down, thinking it was the map to freedom, not knowing it led straight into the slaughterhouse.It's time we burned that blueprint—and built our own.

The School-to-Prison Pipeline:

They started us early. Told us to sit still. Follow rules. Don't question. Color inside the lines. That wasn't education. That was conditioning.Memorize. Obey. Consume.

We learned about Christopher Columbus but not Fred Hampton. Learned calculus but not credit scores. They taught us how to pledge allegiance—but not how to build generational wealth.Why?Because smart slaves are a threat. But obedient ones? Profitable.Debt Is Their Favorite Weapon

Student loans. Credit cards. Car notes. Payday loans. Rent-to-own. Layaway.

They made debt normal. Sexy even.

But debt ain't just financial. It's spiritual. It keeps you in fear. Keeps you hustling backwards. Keeps you distracted. Keeps you from thinking about liberation.

Ever notice how every system in this country is built on you owing them?

You owe taxes. You owe interest. You owe time. You owe loyalty. You owe silence.

But what do they owe you?

Breaking the Cycle: The New Blueprint

Alright, so let's flip it. Let's build a new framework. Not some dreamland fantasy—but a street-level strategy. Here's how we start:

1. Financial Sovereignty Starts with OwnershipForget net worth. Let's talk about ownership.Own your skills.your time.your labor.your story.Start side hustles. Sell knowledge. Monetize creativity. Rent out nothing—own everything. And if you can't own one? Collaborate. Co-ops. Family trusts. Barter networks.No more begging banks. Be the bank.Generational Wealth Ain't Just MoneyYou know what the real inheritance isLand.Knowledge.Mental health.Spiritual armor.Games passed down from your pops, your mama, your tribe.Teach your kids about compound interest and character. Teach them about credit and cultural roots. Give them survival skills and self-respect.

Forget leaving behind cars and Jordans. Leave behind principles, legacy, and options.. Reject the Fake American DreamThe house with the white picket fence? That's a trap too. Property taxes. HOA fees. 30-year mortgages that outlive your marriage. They told you owning a home was the dream. But in many cases, the home owns you.Don't buy symbols. Buy freedom.Freedom doesn't come with granite countertops and three-car garages. It comes with choice. It comes with not needing permission to live your life.

Digital Hustles, Real Returns

This the digital age, and if you ain't making money online, you're a tourist in your own economy.

Get in the game:Sell ebooks. Teach courses.Create a YouTube channel.

Drop shipping. Affiliate marketing. Print-on-demand.NFTs? Maybe. But make it mean something.AI tools? Master them before they replace you.

Don't just consume the internet—capitalize on it.You can't beat the system by begging. You beat it by building your own.

Ancestral Wisdom: Old Keys Still Open DoorsYour great-grandma had no WiFi. No crypto. But she survived.

She knew how to:Grow food.Heal with herbs.Stretch a dollar.Raise kids on principles, not tablets.

That's power.This chapter ain't just about looking forward—it's about looking back too. Our ancestors built pyramids. Raised nations. Defied empires. You think they can't teach us how to escape this new plantation?Listen to the whispers of the old souls.They're saying: "Unlearn. Rebuild. Rise."The Hustle vs. The Harvest

They got you in hustle mode. 24/7. Grind till you die.Nah.We need to shift from hustle to harvest. Hustle builds. Harvest sustains. The key? Systems.

Set up income streams that work while you sleep. Learn automation. Learn delegation. Learn how to scale.If your money stops when you stop, that ain't wealth. That's slavery with extra steps.Spiritual Game Plan: Protect the MindThe real war ain't for your money. It's for your mindset.

You must:Guard your energy.Audit your circle.Kill comparison.Cultivate stillness.

Stay prayed up, meditated, and mentally strapped.This world will drown you in noise. In fear. In algorithmic confusion. Learn how to unplug. To hear yourself. To hear the truth.Because if you don't own your mind, someone else will.Rituals of Power: Everyday ResistanceLet's get practical.Use cash. Often.Shop local. Support independent creators.

Avoid apps that track everything.

Turn off push notifications. Turn on intuition.Study history daily. Study finance weekly. Study yourself always.

These are rituals. Not tasks. These are your rebellion.Final Charge: From Pawn to PowerLet's be real. Most of us were born into a rigged game.But that doesn't mean we gotta die in it.

Somewhere between the bills, the heartbreak, the betrayals, the missed chances, and the long nights—we forgot that we were royalty. Not peasants.

So let this chapter be your mirror.

You are not poor. You are not broken. You are not helpless.You are a sleeping giant.

And this world? This rigged-ass system?

It should be scared.Because you just woke up.

—-Chapter 4: Debt Is the New Chains:

How They Keep You Enslaved with a Smile Welcome to the plantation of the 21st century. There are no whips, no overseers shouting orders in fields. Today, the lash is credit. The cotton is your labor. The plantation is your 30-year mortgage, your student loans, your credit card debt. And the master? The banking system, polished in marble and smiling behind a suit.Let's be real: slavery never ended. It evolved.We traded in chains for contracts. Instead of auction blocks, we've got FICO scores. Instead of shackles, we've got monthly payments. They don't need to keep you in a cage if you keep yourself there voluntarily—hooked on a lifestyle that demands you work until death to afford a fleeting sense of freedom.

—-

The Birth of Debt SlaveryIt starts early. High school feeds you this fantasy: go to college, get a degree, and the world opens up. But here's the truth—they've turned education into a debt trap. A 17-year-old can't legally buy a bottle of wine, but they can sign a $200,000 loan that'll follow them like a shadow for life. And they call that "opportunity."

You walk across that graduation stage with a cap, a gown, and a chain invisible to most—a student loan servicer licking their lips. You enter adulthood already behind, already a prisoner to interest rates you didn't even understand when you signed the papers.

Now you're in the workforce, trying to keep up. You finance a car to get to work. Swipe a card to cover groceries. Get a mortgage because you were told rent is throwing money away. And slowly, the debt piles up—not just the money you owe, but the mental weight, the anxiety, the fear.

It's not just financial anymore. It's spiritual. Psychological. Existential.

You don't own your time—you rent it to survive.The Myth of Good Debt

Ever hear a banker say, "Not all debt is bad"? That's like a dealer saying, "Not all drugs are addictive."They'll tell you mortgages build equity. Student loans are an investment. Business loans create opportunity. But what they don't say is this: every form of debt is a contract of control. You don't move freely when you owe. You don't speak freely when your livelihood is leveraged. You don't live freely when your life is collateral.

The so-called American Dream is built on debt. A house you don't really own until you're 60. A car you barely afford. A degree that doesn't guarantee a job. This dream? It's a trap wrapped in patriotic ribbon.

—-

Credit Scores: Your Economic Collar

Let's talk about FICO scores—the secret handshake of the money class. Your worth, boiled down to three numbers, judged by banks and corporations who get to determine whether you deserve to live with dignity.Pay your bills late? Lose points. Use too much of your credit line? Lose points. Ask for help? Lose points. But you know who doesn't get scored? The billionaires. The corporations. The politicians.

FICO isn't about trust. It's about compliance.They say it rewards "good behavior," but what they mean is obedient behavior. Quiet workers who keep the machine running. You want a home? A car? A business? Play nice. Smile while you sink.

—-

The Interest Trap: The Real Thieves Wear TiesHere's where the heist goes next-level: interest.Let's say you borrow $200,000 for a home. At 6% over 30 years, you end up paying back over $430,000. That's more than double what the house is worth. And who gets that extra $230K? The bank. For what? For typing numbers into a computer. They didn't build the house. They didn't paint it. They didn't clean it. They just loaned you a ghost.

Now multiply that by millions of people doing the same thing. That's trillions in profit—off of air.Credit card companies are even worse. APRs hitting 29.99% while they market rewards like it's a game. "Cash back! Travel points!" All while they bleed you for missing a payment by one day. It's legalized loan sharking, sanitized for suburban life.

—-

Consumerism: The Velvet Rope of the Debt DungeonThey don't even have to force us into debt anymore. They've trained us to beg for it. Flashy commercials. Influencer culture. "Treat yourself" mantras. They sell us comfort, status, convenience—and we sign up gladly, not realizing we're volunteering for bondage.

You don't need that $80,000 SUV. You were convinced you did. You don't need that designer bag. You were programmed to crave it. They've merged capitalism with psychology. Retail therapy is the new worship. And the gods? Visa, Amex, Chase.They dress the cage in luxury. So we decorate it ourselves.

—-

The Generational Curse: Born in Debt, Die in DebtHere's the real tragedy: we pass these chains down like inheritance.

Our kids are born into our debt systems—our mortgages, our car notes, our belief in the system. We raise them to believe credit is power. That a high-paying job is success. That buying a house means you made it.

But we're just teaching them how to walk in circles. Chase paper. Serve the system. Retire broken.True generational wealth isn't just about money—it's about breaking the mindset.

—-

Escaping the Matrix: How to Break Free

Alright, enough doom. Let's talk about strategy.

Step one: Get angry. Anger is fuel. Use it to wake up, not to wallow.Step two: Get educated. Read books. Watch the moves of people who broke out. Learn the rules so you can break them with precision.

Step three: Get lean. Cut the fat. Cut the noise. Stop buying crap to impress people who don't even like you. Build cash flow, not clout.Step four: Get ownership. Own your time. Your business. Your content. Your brand. Real freedom starts when no one can fire you.Step five: Get bold. Start the side hustle. Say no to debt traps. Live below your means so you can rise above your limits.

—-

Final Word: Debt Doesn't Define You

Debt may be their weapon, but knowledge is your shield.You are not your credit score. You are not your loan balance. You are not a cog in their profit machine. You are the engine. You are the storm. And storms don't ask permission—they break chains.

Chapter 5: The Miseducation Trap

Welcome back to The Money Book. You made it this far, and now we need to pull back another layer of the illusion. You ever wonder why school didn't teach you about taxes, credit, compound interest, investing, or who the hell the Rothschilds even are? It wasn't an oversight. It was by design.

Because if knowledge is power, then the first step to keeping you powerless is feeding you junk information.

Let's call it what it is: school is a state-sponsored factory meant to produce obedient workers, not free thinkers. You were never meant to become wealthy, woke, or dangerous. You were meant to clock in, keep your head down, and retire at 65—hopefully too tired to riot.

—-

The Curriculum of Control

They teach you algebra but not how a mortgage works. Geometry but not how to read a lease. They make you memorize the dates of old wars but never the names of the families funding both sides.

Let's be real: the average high school graduate knows how to write a five-paragraph essay about Macbeth, but can't explain how compound interest works, how to build credit, or what inflation actually is.Why?Because a system built on control can't afford a generation that knows how to escape it.

Instead, we were taught to pledge allegiance. To sit still. To raise our hands to speak. To ask for permission to piss. That ain't education. That's training. And what were we being trained for?

A life of silent obedience.

—-

Enter the Rothschilds: The Hidden CurriculumNow let's talk about what school really didn't teach us—like the Rothschild family. You ever wonder how one family, for centuries, has maintained influence over global banking systems? You won't find that in your social studies textbook.

The Rothschilds built their empire in the shadows of European royalty. While empires rose and fell, the Rothschilds played chess with nations. Wars? They financed both sides. Revolutions? They insured their own interests.

They understood something crucial: whoever controls the money, controls the narrative.

So while you were reciting the Pythagorean theorem, they were buying central banks. While you were learning about George Washington's cherry tree, they were creating the Bank of England, the IMF, and influencing the World Bank.

You were taught to salute flags. They were printing the money your government had to borrow.The Real Subjects They Kept From UsLet's break down the curriculum we should have had: Financial Literacy 101: How money works, the history of the dollar, inflation, fiat currency.

Credit Game: How credit scores work, how to build them, how they control your life.

Debt Awareness: Student loans, car loans, credit cards, and how debt is the modern-day plantation.

Entrepreneurship Basics: How to start a business, register an LLC, pay taxes like the rich.Power Structures: Who controls what, from the Federal Reserve to global banking cartels.Propaganda Detection: How media shapes perception, sells you fear, and keeps you docile.But instead we got: Standardized Tests: To measure compliance.Useless Memorization: To reward short-term recall.Historical Lies: Sanitized stories to hide colonialism, genocide, and economic slavery.See the play?

—-

The Debt Pipeline

Here's how the system flows:

1. Underfunded Schools in poor communities push low expectations and minimal skills.

2. Student Loans are marketed as your golden ticket out.

3. College Debt chains you before you even earn your first dollar.

4. Graduation drops you into a market controlled by mega-corps and low wages.

5. Lifestyle Creep (thanks to social media) pushes you to buy what you can't afford.

6. Debt Spiral begins.

And it started in first grade. That's the long con.

—-

Who Owns the Schools?Let's go deeper. Education systems are tied to government funding. Government borrowing comes from central banks. And central banks? Not as public as they seem.

The Federal Reserve is a "private-public" institution. Its board is heavily influenced by banking elites. And while it claims to serve the public, its actions repeatedly bail out billionaires, not students drowning in debt.

Now ask yourself: if the banks benefit from mass debt, why would they ever allow schools to teach kids how to escape it?

They wouldn't. And they haven't.

—-

Break the SpellThe first step to freedom is realizing you were never free. The second step? Unlearning the lies they fed you.Here's what you do:Read books they don't assign.Learn about money like your life depends on it—because it does.

Study taxes, wealth-building, and the psychology of poverty.Build skills, not just degrees.Question every "fact" that comes without a source.

—-

Conclusion: Rewrite the Curriculum

If this chapter made you mad, good.

That rage is fuel.You were trained to be a cog in a machine that prints billionaires and buries the rest. But machines break. Empires fall. And minds, once awakened, don't go back to sleep.

So start writing your own curriculum. One based on freedom, facts, and fire. They had their turn teaching us. Now it's our turn to teach each other.

—-

Chapter 6: The Invisible Empire – Banking Cartels and the Bloodlines of Control

They don't teach you this in school. That's by design.You get taught about George Washington chopping down a cherry tree—but not about Mayer Amschel Rothschild funding empires and revolutions. They give you Pythagorean theorems but never show you how compound interest enslaves nations. You memorize presidents, but they never mention the private families who own the central banks. Why?

Because if you knew who printed the money, you'd stop worshiping the ones who spent it.Let's talk about them—the shadow kings. The banking cartel. The real "Illuminati" of finance.

—-

It Started in Frankfurt: The Rothschild Genesis Mayer Amschel Rothschild—remember the name. Not a king. Not a general. Just a coin dealer from Frankfurt who figured out the ultimate cheat code: control the money, and you control the world.

He had five sons. Send them out like chess pieces across Europe—London, Paris, Vienna, Naples, Frankfurt. Each one planted like a financial seed. Each one linked by blood, marriage, and mission.

Their strategy? Bankroll both sides of every war. Napoleon? Funded. The British fighting him? Also funded. You think loyalty was to any flag? No. Loyalty was to profit. War is the most profitable business on Earth, and the Rothschilds mastered the model.

After the Battle of Waterloo, Nathan Rothschild in London used early intel to flip the entire British economy. He pretended to sell off his government bonds, making others panic and sell too. Once prices bottomed, he bought them all back—owning the lion's share of Britain's debt. In a single day, he went from rich to mythic.That was the blueprint.

—-

From Rothschild to Rockefeller – The American Branch of the Cartel

As Europe got stitched up by the Rothschild dynasty, America was next.

Enter John D. Rockefeller.He didn't just build Standard Oil—he built the illusion of corporate dominance. But the real prize wasn't oil. It was the banks. It was an influence. It was the ability to fund wars, rewrite education, and manufacture medicine—all through nonprofit foundations that looked like charity, but operated like empires.Fast-forward to 1913. A date every American should tattoo on their soul.

—-

The Federal Reserve Coup

While you were learning about apple pies and liberty bells, the real coup went down on Jekyll Island. A secret meeting—attended by bankers like Paul Warburg (connected to the Rothschilds), Nelson Aldrich, and a few Wall Street elite—plotted out a central banking system that would hand control of America's money to a private cartel.And Congress? Bought and sold.They passed the Federal Reserve Act on December 23, 1913, while most lawmakers were home for Christmas.

Since then, the U.S. dollar hasn't belonged to the people. It belongs to the Fed. And guess what? The Federal Reserve isn't federal, and it holds no reserves.

It's a privately owned bank, masquerading as a government institution.They print the money. They set the rates. They control inflation. They decide recessions.

And every dollar they lend? Comes with interest.Which means every dollar in your pocket is a debt to the Fed.You were born into it. They didn't ask for your consent.

—-

IMF, World Bank, and the Global Debt MachineBut the cartel didn't stop at America.After World War II, they expanded—through the International Monetary Fund (IMF) and World Bank. These institutions were framed as global helpers, but their real role was to trap nations in debt.

They'd give poor countries massive loans, with strings attached—privatize your utilities, let our corporations in, cut social services. Once the country defaults (because the loans are designed to be impossible to repay), the cartel seizes land, resources, and influence.

It's colonialism in a three-piece suit.

From Jamaica to Ghana to Argentina—this is how empires are built in the 21st century. Not with armies. With banks.p pop

—-

Bank for International Settlements – The Central Bank of Central Banks

Have you ever heard of the BIS?Didn't think so.

The Bank for International Settlements in Basel, Switzerland is the godfather of them all. It's where central banks—like the Fed, the Bank of England, the European Central Bank—go to coordinate. No media. No public oversight. Just meetings behind closed doors.

They call themselves a "banker's bank." But in reality, they're the command center of global monetary policy. If the world economy had a Death Star, it would look a lot like BIS.

—-

Money Magic: Fractional Reserve Lending and the Creation of Currency

Now here's the real voodoo.Banks don't just hold your money—they create money from nothing. It's called fractional reserve banking.

Let's say you deposit $1,000 into a bank. That bank is only required to hold a fraction of it—say, 10%—as reserves. The rest? They loan it out. So they lend $900 to someone else. That person deposits it, and boom—they loan out 90% of that. Over and over, the cycle continues.

From your $1,000, banks can create $9,000 or more in new money—money that never physically existed.

That's how inflation gets baked into the system. That's why your rent keeps going up. That's why the dollar you saved yesterday buys less tomorrow.

They dilute the pool, while hoarding the faucet.

—-

The Media Is Their Megaphone

Think the news will tell you this? Nah.

Most mainstream outlets are owned by six corporations—all funded or influenced by banking money. They push stock market optimism while quietly preparing you for the next crash.

They talk about celebrities and culture wars while ignoring the billion-dollar bailouts happening behind the scenes. They tell you crypto is dangerous while JPMorgan and BlackRock build their own blockchain systems.

Propaganda is more profitable than truth.

—-

Crypto, CBDCs, and the New Chains of Control You thought Bitcoin was the answer? Maybe.But the cartel saw it coming. That's why they're rolling out Central Bank Digital Currencies (CBDCs). With CBDCs, the government (and its banking overlords) can track every transaction. Every dime. Every dollar. Programmable money that can be turned off, geo-fenced, or expired.They say it's for convenience.But it's really about control.

Imagine your social media behavior affecting your access to cash. Imagine missing a payment and your money getting frozen. Imagine dissent costing you your wallet.That's not freedom. That's a financial prison disguised as progress.

—-

How They Keep You Blind: Education, Distraction, and Debt Ask yourself: Why don't schools teach any of this?

Because the system isn't designed to create free thinkers—it's built to produce obedient workers. You were trained to follow, not question. To memorize, not analyze.The average graduate leaves school knowing how to take a test—but not how to read a bank statement. They can diagram a sentence but can't understand a mortgage contract. They know Shakespeare but not how compound interest turns a $1,000 credit card into a $5,000 nightmare.It's intentional.

Financial illiteracy keeps the masses working for crumbs while the elite feast unseen.

—-

Breaking the Spell: What You Can Do

This chapter ain't about hopelessness. It's about awakening.The first step? Understand the game. Once you see the strings, you stop being a puppet. Educate yourself on how money is made. Learn about inflation. Study how banks operate. Dig into the BIS, IMF, and Federal Reserve. Ask the forbidden questions.

Next? Get off their plantation.

Start your own business. Use crypto wisely (outside of the centralized systems). Buy assets, not liabilities. Get your community financially literate. Teach your kids the truth. Create networks of trust that don't rely on their paper chains.The cartel counts on our ignorance. So feed your mind like your life depends on it—because it does.

—-

Final Thought: They Print the Money, But We Create the Value

At the end of the day, money is just belief. It's paper. Pixels. Promises.

What gives it power is you—your sweat, your labor, your genius, your attention.

They print it.We make it real.

It's time to flip the table, burn the rulebook, and remember this: the banking cartel is strong—but an awakened person is stronger.Awesome! Let's dive into it.

Chapter 8: The Rise of the Global Surveillance State

—-

Introduction: The Eyes of the World

In today's hyper-connected world, where every interaction, transaction, and communication is logged, the boundaries between personal freedom and government control have begun to blur. As AI continues to grow in power and influence, the tools used by global elites to manipulate and control society are becoming increasingly sophisticated. Behind the scenes, entities like the Rothschild family, the Rockefellers, and other banking dynasties are silently orchestrating a world where surveillance is ubiquitous and personal autonomy is a thing of the past. This chapter will explore how AI is fueling the rise of the global surveillance state, the pivotal role of tech giants and powerful banking cartels, and the implications for freedom and privacy.

The Mechanics of Surveillance: A Web of EyesThe centralization of surveillance power is not just a future threat; it's a present-day reality. Governments, corporations, and even non-state actors are harnessing the capabilities of AI to monitor and control every aspect of our lives. The rise of AI-powered technologies like facial recognition, biometric tracking, and mass data collection has made it easier than ever for the state to watch its citizens. But AI is not the only force at play here. There is a deeper, more insidious force: the global banking cartel.

The Rothschilds, Rockefellers, and their financial allies have long understood that control over money and resources is control over society. As we shift towards a digital economy, these banking families are positioning themselves at the helm of a new financial world order, one where every transaction, every movement, and every decision is tracked, analyzed, and controlled by AI.Rothschild and Rockefeller InfluenceHistorically, the Rothschild and Rockefeller families have wielded significant influence in shaping global financial and political systems. From funding wars to manipulating stock markets, these families have consistently used their wealth and power to control global economies. But in the age of AI, their power is no longer limited to just economic control—it extends into the realm of surveillance and information.

The Rothschild banking empire, for example, is rumored to have deep ties with tech giants and government intelligence agencies, creating an intricate web of financial and digital surveillance. The Rothschilds' connections with the Israeli military and its cutting-edge cybersecurity operations give them an unparalleled advantage in the world of AI surveillance. Meanwhile, the Rockefellers, with their involvement in international organizations like the United Nations and the World Economic Forum, have pushed for global policies that favor the centralization of power, including the rise of digital currencies and smart cities.

The Role of Tech Giants: The Silicon Valley CartelIf the Rothschilds and Rockefellers are the puppet masters, then tech giants like Google, Facebook, Amazon, and Apple are their trusted hands, pulling the strings of our digital lives. These companies hold vast amounts of personal data on billions of people across the globe, and they are deeply intertwined with governments in ways that are often invisible to the public eye.

For instance, Google's parent company, Alphabet, has close ties to the U.S. military and intelligence agencies, with projects like Google's AI-driven Project Maven and their work on drone technology. Facebook has become an essential tool for global surveillance, with its facial recognition software, the vast network of data it collects, and its integration with government systems. Amazon, meanwhile, provides the backbone of cloud storage through AWS, which is used by both private companies and government agencies for data storage and analysis.

These corporations are not just passive players—they are active participants in the creation of the surveillance state. The data they collect is used not only to sell products but also to track, predict, and influence behaviors, solidifying the control that the banking cartels and governments have over their citizens.

Smart Cities: The Digital Panopticon

One of the most disturbing developments in the rise of the surveillance state is the creation of smart cities—urban environments equipped with a vast array of sensors, cameras, and AI-driven technologies that monitor everything from traffic patterns to individual movements. These cities are being marketed as the future of urban living, promising efficiency, sustainability, and safety. However, the reality is that they represent a massive step toward total surveillance.

Cities like Singapore and Beijing have already implemented smart city technologies, with facial recognition systems used to track and control their populations. The Chinese government has built an entire surveillance apparatus around its Social Credit System, where AI monitors citizens' behavior, rewarding compliance and punishing dissent. This is the model that many Western cities are striving to emulate.

In the U.S., cities like New York, Los Angeles, and San Francisco are beginning to adopt AI-powered surveillance systems under the guise of improving public safety. These systems include things like automatic license plate readers, surveillance cameras in public spaces, and even predictive policing algorithms that forecast where crimes are most likely to occur.

While these smart city technologies are sold to the public as safety measures, they also pave the way for an ever-tightening digital prison, where every aspect of a citizen's life is monitored, analyzed, and controlled.AI and Predictive Policing: The Orwellian Future of Law Enforcement

One of the most troubling uses of AI in the surveillance state is predictive policing, where algorithms are used to predict who is most likely to commit a crime. This system is already in place in cities across the U.S., where data collected from previous arrests, social media, and even surveillance footage is fed into an algorithm that then predicts future criminal behavior.

However, this technology has significant flaws. The data used to train these algorithms is often biased, leading to disproportionately high rates of surveillance in minority communities. As AI becomes more deeply entrenched in policing, it's clear that it will be used not just to identify criminals, but to enforce conformity. Those who challenge the system—be it through protest, dissent, or even political disagreement—will find themselves increasingly monitored and targeted.The Financial Implications of AI Surveillance

At the heart of the surveillance state lies a massive financial engine. As AI-driven systems continue to expand, they are increasingly being integrated into the global financial system. The introduction of Central Bank Digital Currencies (CBDCs) is one of the most significant developments in this area. These digital currencies, controlled by central banks and powered by AI algorithms, represent a massive shift in global finance.

CBDCs will allow governments and financial institutions to track every transaction, control the money supply, and even restrict access to funds for individuals deemed to be "undesirable." The introduction of CBDCs, coupled with AI, will give global elites unprecedented power over the global economy, ensuring that they control not just the money, but the very movement of capital.

Conclusion: The Dangers of a Digital DictatorshipThe rise of the global surveillance state is not just a theoretical future—it's happening right now. As AI continues to develop and as tech giants and banking cartels consolidate power, the world is rapidly moving toward a system where personal autonomy is an illusion. The surveillance state is becoming increasingly difficult to escape, with our every move tracked, analyzed, and controlled.

But this doesn't have to be our future. By understanding the forces at play and taking steps to push back against the rise of AI-driven control, we can still reclaim our freedom. In the next chapter, we'll dive deeper into the role of Central Bank Digital Currencies (CBDCs) and how they are poised to reshape the global financial system and further entrench the power of the elites.

—-

Chapter 7: The Digital Prison – How AI Is Tightening the Chains

If you're still thinking about the future, you're already behind. Because the future isn't some far-off dream anymore. It's here—now. And the architects of this brave new world are not the ones you think. It's the same old faces—hidden in plain sight—driving us into a digital prison.

The tools of this prison? Artificial Intelligence.At its surface, AI seems like a gift. Convenience, efficiency, speed. But when you peel back the layers, you'll find that AI is the lock and key holding us in a cage we can't see, but can feel every day.

—-

The Illusion of Convenience

Think about your day-to-day life. Your phone buzzes with notifications, apps recommend what you should do, buy, watch, and who you should be friends with. We've all become so used to it that it's hard to even remember a time when life wasn't shaped by this algorithmic guidance.But this is where they start to get you. AI isn't just here to make life easier. It's here to make you predictable. It's here to make you trackable. Your likes, dislikes, buying habits, your emotional triggers—everything you do online is scrutinized, stored, and cataloged.

This might sound like the stuff of conspiracy theories, but it's not. It's the foundation of the digital age. The more you feed into it, the more the system learns about you. It knows what you like, what you need, and more importantly, it can predict what you'll do next.

How does this help the powers that be? Simple. They can use this information to shape your behavior. To guide you into purchasing things, adopting opinions, and staying inside an echo chamber where you only hear things that reinforce what you already believe.What if I told you this is just the beginning? That the real impact is deeper—much deeper.

—-

AI and the Shadow Over Privacy

We've been told that our data is just numbers, a simple set of information that helps companies serve us better. But privacy is something we used to value, something we assumed was ours by default. Now? It's a luxury.

Governments and corporations aren't just collecting your data—they're using it against you. The ultimate goal isn't just marketing. It's surveillance. It's power.

We see it everywhere now, in the form of facial recognition, voice tracking, location monitoring, and predictive algorithms that tell us what we want to buy before we even know we want it. But what happens when AI's ability to predict our behavior gets so advanced that it begins to track not only our purchases but our thoughts, our interactions, our beliefs?

What if we lived in a world where AI could predict when you'd break the law, when you'd join a protest, or when you'd speak out against the system?

The system already knows how you'll react in almost every situation. Predictive policing is the next step—AI-powered surveillance designed to anticipate criminal activity before it happens. It's already being tested in cities around the world, where police departments use AI to scan social media, track movements, and predict who might be involved in criminal activity.

This isn't science fiction. This is reality. And the question is: What happens when this technology is used not just to catch criminals, but to control dissent?

—-

The Social Credit System: A Blueprint for Global Control

China's Social Credit System is often discussed as a horrifying glimpse of the future. The system tracks everything citizens do: their online behavior, their purchases, their social interactions, and even their personal opinions. If you criticize the government or get caught in an undesirable act, your score drops. You lose privileges—like access to transportation, education, or even your job.

Sounds like a dystopian nightmare, right?

But that's only part of the picture.

China's social credit system is the prototype for what could be a global norm. AI, in collaboration with data mining and surveillance, could soon be the global enforcer of a new world order. Imagine a world where your every move is tracked, and your worth is not just based on your actions, but your thoughts and beliefs. Social credit will soon be the measure of your value to the system—and it's just one step away from being used to create a global control system.

AI will know more about you than your closest friends and family. It will dictate your financial access, your social standing, and even your ability to move through the world. It will keep you locked in a cage of convenience, where you are free to make choices—so long as they align with the machine's predictions.

—-

The Real Danger: AI in the Financial System

But it gets even more chilling. We're not just talking about the control of your personal information or social behavior. AI is already starting to infiltrate the financial system.It's the perfect storm: AI-powered financial algorithms, the rise of Central Bank Digital Currencies (CBDCs), and a world moving toward a cashless society.

With AI embedded in the monetary system, your entire financial life could be controlled, manipulated, and restricted based on a set of invisible parameters. Banks already use AI to track your spending habits, offer personalized loans, and even dictate the terms of your credit. But what if that AI was also used to punish you for actions outside of the system's control?

A protest against a corporation or an unpopular opinion could result in you being cut off from access to funds or credit. Your social score could determine your financial worth, determining what loans you can take, what businesses you can work with, and even what services you're eligible for.

Your wealth, your livelihood, and your ability to thrive could be placed in the hands of algorithms that you can't control. And if they want to lock you down—financially, socially, or even physically—AI has the power to do just that.

—-

AI and the Death of Personal Freedom

What does this mean for personal freedom? If we allow this system to evolve unchecked, AI will strip away every last vestige of individuality. It will determine your thoughts, your actions, your financial situation, and your place in society.

We'll be locked—not by physical walls, but by a web of ones and zeros, tracking our every movement, decision, and belief.

And the scariest part? We won't even realize it until it's too late.

In the not-too-distant future, your entire life could be controlled by AI. A system that tells you where to go, what to buy, what to think, and what to say.

And as more power consolidates, and more data accumulates, it will become harder and harder to escape. The walls are closing in, tighter and tighter, until we're all trapped.

—-

The Path to Freedom: Disconnect and Reclaim

So, what can we do? How do we break free from this tightening grip?

The first step is simple: awareness. We have to understand the game before we can change the rules. The more people understand how AI is being used to control their lives, the harder it will be for these systems to keep operating unchecked.

The second step is to disconnect. We need to reclaim our privacy, limit the data we give out, and find alternative ways to interact with the world. Use privacy tools, encrypted communication, and start supporting decentralized systems that offer more control over our personal data.

And finally, we have to build new systems—new ways to interact with the world without the constant surveillance, manipulation, and control of AI. We can create communities outside of the control structures, and we can use technology to reclaim the freedom that is rightfully ours.

It won't be easy. The system is powerful, and its reach is vast. But we're not helpless. The digital chains may be tightening, but if we act now, we can break them before they completely bind us.

—-

Conclusion:

AI may have been sold to us as the next great leap forward, but in reality, it's just another tool in a long history of oppression and control. The more we feed into it, the more we lose ourselves. If we want to maintain our freedom, we need to start pushing back, now. The question is: will we choose to wake up before it's too late, or will we let AI lock us in forever?

—-

Chapter 9: The Digital Trap – CBDCs, Social Credit, and the Future of Freedom

They told you cash was dirty. That digital was safer. That convenience is king.

And while you were busy tapping your phone to pay for groceries, a new kind of prison was being built around you—one swipe at a time.This chapter ain't afraid of porn. It's a fact. Cold, sharp, unapologetic.

Because the next evolution of money isn't just about currency—it's about control.

—-

From Paper to Programs: The Death of Cash Let's start with a fact: over 90% of the world's money is already digital. It doesn't exist as coins or bills. It's just numbers on a screen. Ones and zeros in a bank's database.You thought you had money? Nah. You have permission to use money, until the system decides otherwise.

The rise of CBDCs—Central Bank Digital Currencies—is the next nail in the coffin. These ain't crypto. They're not Bitcoin. They're not decentralized. They're programmable, trackable, and revocable—money with strings attached.

Imagine this:Your paycheck arrives... but it expires in 30 days if you don't spend it.

Your "carbon footprint" was too high this month? Sorry, you can't book that flight.

Said something spicy on social media? Funds frozen for violating "terms of service."Missed a vaccine mandate? No access to public transit. No rent payment.

That's not hypothetical. That's the direction we're headed.In 2023, over 100 countries were piloting or researching CBDCs. China's already running live trials of its digital yuan, complete with expiry dates and purchase restrictions. Europe's rolling out the "Digital Euro." The U.S.? Quietly testing FedNow, the infrastructure for instant settlement—and total oversight.

This is the endgame of the banking cartel.

—-

The Money Police: How Programmable Currency Enforces Obedience

The Rothschilds once said, "Permit me to issue and control the money of a nation, and I care not who makes its laws."

Now imagine not just issuing the money—but controlling how it's spent.

CBDCs give central banks god-mode:

Geofencing: Your money only works in authorized zones.Time limits: Stimulus funds that vanish if you don't spend fast enough.Blacklist integration: A few keystrokes and poof—you're unbanked.

This ain't some Orwellian future—it's the present. They've just wrapped it in the language of "efficiency" and "safety."

And behind it all?The same banking cartel that funded both sides of every major war, from Napoleon to Iraq. The same hands behind the IMF, World Bank, BIS, and every modern financial chokehold.

These banks don't serve people. They serve power.

—-

The Social Credit CageLet's link it up.

Digital money is the rails.Social credit is the train.China's already there. Citizens are scored like Uber drivers—good behavior earns perks, bad behavior gets punished. Post something anti-government? Can't buy a plane ticket. Miss a bill? Your kid can't go to a good school. Date someone with a low score? Your rating drops.

Now bring that west. They'll never call it "social credit" here. They'll call it ESG compliance, carbon limits, health passports, or community trust scores.

But it all leads to the same place: behavioral control through economic pressure.You don't need a boot on your neck if your wallet is chained to obedience.

—-

The Disappearing Middle Class

While the elite stack trillions, the middle class is getting squeezed like a lemon in a Coke bottle.Inflation isn't a fluke—it's financial warfare.Your dollars are worth less. Your savings are melting. Home ownership? Out of reach. College? A debt trap. Healthcare? A luxury.This is by design.They want two classes:

The Owners: Corporations, billionaires, AI overlords.The Owned: You, your kids, your future.Middle class means mobility. It means you can escape. You can question. You can build.So they're gutting it. Erasing it. Locking you into a gig economy with no benefits and no bargaining power. Making you depend on their system to survive.

—-

AI as the Gatekeeper of Finance

Artificial intelligence ain't coming for your job. It already did.It's also coming for your financial freedom.Banks are already using AI to:Approve or deny loans in milliseconds.Flag "suspicious" behavior for investigation.Monitor your spending patterns for marketing... or manipulation.

AI will soon run the financial system top to bottom. That means bias on steroids. That means total automation of exclusion. That means no appeal when a bot decides you're a threat.Worse? The same AI will drive predictive policing, credit scoring, risk assessment, and insurance premiums.

What you buy, where you go, who you talk to—it's all data.And your data is their leash.

—-

The Rothschild Legacy: Still Pulling Strings

Let's not forget who built this web.

The Rothschild banking dynasty didn't just dominate European finance—they designed the game. They lent money to monarchs, funded wars, bought newspapers, and backed both empires and revolutions.Their philosophy?

"The few who understand the system will either be so interested in its profits or so dependent on its favors that there will be no opposition."Sound familiar?

Their influence lives on through the IMF, World Bank, central banks, and elite institutions. You don't see the Rothschild name in headlines anymore—but their blueprint is alive and thriving.

It's a pyramid scheme wrapped in a flag.

—-

This Ain't Just About Money is the front.

The real play is submission.When you can't eat without swiping a card, when you can't travel without a QR code, when you can't speak without risking de-banking—you're not free. You're pleased. Licensed to exist.The goal? A population so micromanaged they police themselves.Every move tracked. Every choice pre-approved. Every deviation punished by silence, censorship, or starvation.The 21st century won't be marked by gulags or chains.

It'll be digital prisons with open doors you're too scared to walk through.

—-

What Can You Do?

You can't vote your way out of a system owned by money.But you can disengage, educate, and build alternatives.Use cash where you can.Stack assets they can't freeze—precious metals, crypto (not CBDC), food, knowledge.Support decentralized platforms.Talk to people. Real talk. Wake them up gently but firmly.

And most of all:Resist the programming.

You are not a node in their network.

You are a soul, a force, a fire.

And once you understand how they've caged your freedom through the illusion of choice and the weaponization of money—you start to become dangerous.

—-

Conclusion: The System's Endgame

The war isn't coming.It's already here.

It's quiet. Polished. Algorithmic. Policed by bots and enforced by policy. Funded by central banks. Wrapped in convenience. Sold as safety.But the truth remains:

Money is the leash. And they're tightening it.But knowledge? That's the knife.

This chapter was your whetstone.

Sharpen up.We're not done.

—-

The future is here. Or at least, it's been here for a while, and most of us have been too caught up in the day-to-day grind to see it coming. Now, the systems that once seemed distant and abstract—banks, corporations, governments—are on the verge of merging into something far more insidious and powerful than we ever imagined.Welcome to Digital Tyranny.

It's a world where your data isn't just tracked; it's monetized. Where algorithms make decisions about your life, your credit, your job prospects, and even your identity. Where the money isn't real—it's all just ones and zeros, flowing through the invisible pipes of the internet, controlled by a select few who pull the strings behind the curtain.The Silent Reign of the Banking Cartel

Before we go any further, let's talk about the Rothschild banking dynasty. To many, they represent the ultimate embodiment of power—an old-money family that controls wealth in ways most can't even comprehend. With their tentacles in everything from central banking to international finance, their reach is unparalleled. The Rothschilds aren't just rich—they are the architects of much of the global financial architecture we see today.

In the modern world, however, the Rothschilds are just the beginning. The financial system, with its roots in the age-old banking cartel, has evolved into something that straddles the digital and physical worlds. And this evolution is exponentially more dangerous.

Consider the Federal Reserve, that colossal institution that has long been a subject of conspiracy and debate. It's often portrayed as a stabilizing force in the U.S. economy, but in reality, it's a tool of the financial elite—those who control the flow of money, interest rates, and credit. The money it prints isn't really money. It's debt. It's a promise to pay, but the debt can never be repaid because it's structured to grow. This system keeps us chasing the impossible dream of wealth while the bankers pull the strings behind closed doors, creating crises, debt, and booms to control the markets, manipulate policy, and consolidate power.

But now, we're entering a new phase in the game—one where digital currencies are pushing the old system into a digital prison, where everyone is monitored and controlled by algorithms, AI, and the invisible hand of the banks.

—-

AI: The New Keeper of Wealth

Let's take a moment to talk about AI—the tool of tomorrow that's already here. AI is changing everything. It's already in our phones, controlling ads, curating our news, and pushing us toward products and services that feed into the system of consumerism.

But AI isn't just a tool for advertising. It's the next frontier for the banking cartel. Central Bank Digital Currencies (CBDCs) are the new wave, and they're being quietly rolled out under the guise of innovation. The idea is simple: a central bank would issue a digital currency that is programmable, traceable, and completely under their control. No more cash under your mattress, no more freedom to move your wealth without leaving a trace. Every transaction you make will be logged. Every purchase, every sale, every exchange will be part of a digital footprint that can be monitored and analyzed.

In theory, this system could make everything "more efficient"—no more middlemen, no more processing fees, faster transactions. But what happens when the same AI that powers these digital currencies is also programmed to limit your access to money, based on what you buy or who you associate with? The rich get richer. The poor get less.

If you think I'm being paranoid, let's look at what's already happening. In China, a social credit system is being implemented, where citizens are rewarded or punished based on their behavior. You can be penalized for something as simple as bad driving, or for speaking out against the government. Your money—your ability to access it—becomes a tool of control, based on your social behavior.

Now, imagine this on a global scale. This is what the banking cartel wants—total control over your spending, your savings, your wealth. They'll know exactly where you're spending your money, and they'll decide who gets to spend and who doesn't.

—-

Data: The True Currency

But AI and digital currencies are just tools—they're part of the greater machine that's already in motion. The real currency in this new world is data.

You think you're free because you're not paying with cash anymore? Wrong. The real payment is in your data. Every time you use your phone, your credit card, your online bank account, you're generating data. Your browsing habits, your purchase history, your location, your social media activity—this is the real currency. This is how they know you.Every company that profits from your data is tied to the banking system. Every time you log on to Facebook or Instagram, every time you make a purchase on Amazon, you're feeding the beast. You're training algorithms that predict your next move, but also feeding them information about your vulnerabilities.

Here's where it gets insidious. Data isn't just information—it's influence. It can be used to manipulate you. Predict your thoughts, your choices, your desires. The same algorithms that recommend products to you are the same ones that could push political propaganda or shape your worldview. They know what makes you tick, and they can use that to control your actions.

The biggest players in the game—Google, Amazon, Facebook—aren't just tech companies. They're banks in disguise. They hold the most valuable commodity in the world today: your data. But there's a twist—while you pay for their services with your attention, your time, and your data, they're getting richer and more powerful. They are feeding off the same capital that the banking cartel is using to shape the global economy. They hold the power to track your every move, not just online, but in the physical world too.

—-

The Money and Power Loop

So, where does this all tie together? It's simple: the control of money isn't about physical cash anymore. It's about controlling the flow of information, data, and transactions.

When you stop thinking of money as just a physical currency, and start thinking of it as a system of control, everything starts to make sense.Think about the latest innovations in quantum computing—the technology that will allow the banking cartel to process data at unprecedented speeds. The moment they tap into quantum power, they will have the ability to control every single aspect of the global financial system, instantly calculating your credit score, your social behavior, and deciding whether or not you can even buy groceries.

Capitalism, as we've known it, is on the verge of being replaced with technocratic feudalism—a world where a handful of Really Good Book

Foreword:

They told you that you were free. That you had choices. That the government exists to protect you, to serve you, to ensure justice for all. But what if I told you that was all bullshit? That the world you live in—the so-called "Land of the Free"—is nothing more than a carefully crafted illusion designed to keep you docile, distracted, and under control?

This book isn't for the weak. It isn't for those who need the comfort of mainstream narratives to sleep at night. This is for the people who already feel that something is wrong—who sense the cracks in the system but have never been able to put their finger on why.

We've been lied to. Manipulated. Programmed. And every time someone gets too close to the truth, they're silenced—one way or another. But the truth doesn't die. It festers. It grows. And today, I'm throwing a match on the pile of lies they've buried us under.

The Blueprint of Control

From the MKUltra mind control experiments to the government's orchestration of 9/11, from Charles Manson as a tool to discredit the counterculture to the flooding of Black communities with heroin and crack to destroy revolutionaries like the Black Panthers—every chapter in this book rips apart the comfortable illusion you've been force-fed.

This isn't just about corruption. Corruption is what happens when a system fails. No, this is something far worse—this is a deliberate, calculated structure of control. The people in power don't make mistakes; they make moves. And every crisis, every scandal, every so-called "terrorist attack" or "drug epidemic" has a purpose—to make sure you stay exactly where they want you: weak, dependent, and scared.

Why This Book Will Piss People Off

This book is going to ruffle feathers, and that's exactly the point. The government, the media, and the corporations—they all rely on your silence. They count on you being too busy, too distracted, too afraid to question anything. They want you fighting over race, gender, and politics so you never look up and realize that they are the ones screwing all of us over.

I'm not here to tell you what to think. I'm here to put the facts in front of you—the declassified documents, the whistleblower testimonies, the hidden reports—and let you see for yourself just how deep the rabbit hole goes.

If you're comfortable with the world as it is, put this book down now. But if you're ready to face the truth—raw, uncut, and in your face—then turn the page.

Chapter 1: The Illusion of Freedom

In the dim light of a world that spins fast on the axis of convenience and complacency, the notion of freedom flutters like a fragile butterfly, its vibrant colors dulled by the cage of societal constructs. Here, within the confines of this narrative, I invite you to peel back the layers of your understanding, to question the very essence of what you believe constitutes freedom. You see, dear reader, freedom is not merely the absence of chains; it is, more often than not, a manufactured illusion. It has been carefully curated by those in power to keep you docile and compliant.

As the author of this exploration, I stand before you—not as an omniscient deity, but as a fellow traveler navigating the treacherous waters of reality. The Government looms large, a specter in the background of everyday life, while the Press, that supposed bastion of truth, plays its role like an actor in a grand theater production. The spotlight may shine brightly on the stage, but what lies behind the curtains is a narrative crafted with meticulous intent, obscured from your view.

Imagine for a moment: You wake up to the blaring sounds of morning news. The familiar voices of anchors nestle into your consciousness, painting a picture of a world where democracy reigns supreme, where your voice matters. Yet, as you sip your coffee and listen, a gnawing feeling stirs within you. Are you truly free, or are you merely a cog in a vast machine—one that thrives on your participation and your belief in a system designed to benefit a select few?

The streets outside your window pulse with life, and yet, they are lined with the shadows of disillusionment. The cars that rush by, the people engrossed in their devices, all seem to be living their lives in a state of blissful ignorance. They are free, or so they think, while the invisible hands of control guide their choices and dictate their actions. It's a dance of illusion, choreographed to perfection, where the audience remains oblivious to the strings pulling at their every move.

You may find yourself wondering, How can this be? The answer lies in a simple truth: the world is not as it seems. The narrative you've been fed—the one that tells you that you have a voice, that you can effect change—is a carefully constructed facade. It is a tool wielded by the Government to maintain its grip on power, and the Press, in turn, serves as its willing accomplice. Together, they create a tapestry of misinformation, woven with threads of selective reporting and sensationalism, designed to distract you from the reality lurking beneath the surface.

Consider the role of the Press. Once heralded as the Fourth Estate, it was meant to act as a watchdog, guarding against tyranny and injustice. But in the age of corporate influence and political patronage, the Press has become a puppet, dancing to the tune of its masters. News cycles churn out stories that captivate and terrify, while the real issues—those that threaten the status quo—are buried beneath a mountain of triviality. The truth is often hidden in plain sight, obscured by the very institutions that claim to uphold it.

In this chapter, we embark on a journey to dissect the illusion of freedom, to strip away the layers of complacency that have been draped over our eyes. As we delve deeper, we will encounter historical events that reveal the lengths to which the Government will go to maintain control. We will examine how the Press has evolved from a source of information to a purveyor of distraction, manipulating narratives to serve the interests of a select few.

But before we proceed, I urge you to engage with this material not as a passive observer but as an active participant in the discourse. Question everything. Challenge your beliefs. The stakes are

high, for the freedom you thought you possessed may be nothing more than an elaborate ruse.

As we traverse this landscape together, let your skepticism be your guide. Allow it to illuminate the shadows where truth hides, and let it empower you to reclaim your understanding of freedom. For it is only through this awakening that we can hope to dismantle the illusion that has entrapped us for far too long.

In the coming pages, I will lay bare the mechanisms of control that have been employed throughout history, revealing how the illusion of freedom has been used as a tool to pacify the masses. Together, we will confront the uncomfortable truths that lie beneath the surface, armed with the knowledge that awareness is the first step toward liberation.

So, let us begin. The journey ahead may be fraught with discomfort, but it is necessary. The illusion of freedom is a powerful adversary, but with each revelation, we draw closer to the reality that awaits us—a reality that is not just ours to discover, but to reclaim.

As the curtain rises on this exploration, I ask you to keep an open mind and a vigilant heart. The stakes are high, and the truth is waiting to be unearthed. Welcome to the beginning of your awakening.

Chapter 2: The Blueprint of Control

The air in the dimly lit room was thick with anticipation, as if the very walls were holding their breath, waiting for the truth to unfold. A single flickering bulb hung from the ceiling, casting shadows that danced across stacks of files and documents, remnants of a history that was both chilling and compelling. In the center of this chaos sat the author, a figure cloaked in the shadows of conspiracy, ready to unveil the intricate web of manipulation spun by those in power.

The Illusion of Security

Imagine a world where every action is monitored, every thought scrutinized, and every dissent silenced. This is not a dystopian fantasy but a reality that has been meticulously orchestrated by the very institutions that claim to protect us. The author leaned closer to the desk, fingers brushing against the yellowed pages of history, each one a testament to the lengths governments would go to maintain control over their citizens.

The events of the past century have laid bare the strategies employed by those in power. From the experimental horrors of MKUltra to the cataclysmic events of September 11, 2001, these moments are not isolated incidents; they are part of a deliberate and calculated blueprint for control. The author sought to expose the dark underbelly of these occurrences, illustrating how fear and manipulation have been wielded as weapons against the populace.

MKUltra: The Dark Arts of Mind Control

Unraveling the narrative of MKUltra was like peeling back the layers of a rotting onion. Each layer revealed a deeper stench of corruption and cruelty. This covert CIA program, initiated in the early 1950s, aimed to develop methods of mind control through a series of unethical experiments on unwitting subjects. The author recalled the testimonies of those who became victims of this insidious program—individuals who lost their grip on reality, who were turned into puppets dancing on the strings of their handlers.

Among the historical figures in this grim saga was Sidney Gottlieb, a CIA operative known as the "Black Sorcerer." He orchestrated experiments involving hallucinogenic drugs, torture, and psychological manipulation, all under the guise of national security. The author's voice dripped with disdain as they recounted Gottlieb's chilling philosophy: "The mind is the battlefield." This sentiment echoed through history, revealing a disturbing truth—the government was willing to sacrifice its own citizens for the sake of power.

The author's tone shifted, growing darker as they delved into the ramifications of MKUltra. This was not merely a story of unethical experimentation; it was a reflection of a society that had allowed its government to overstep its bounds. Citizens had become mere pawns in a game of chess, manipulated by those who wielded authority without accountability. The urgency in the author's narrative was palpable, pushing readers to confront the uncomfortable reality that they, too, could be subjected to such control.

The Orchestration of 9/11

Just as the legacy of MKUltra had left a scar on the American psyche, the events of 9/11 would forever change the trajectory of global politics. The author navigated through the fog of confusion

and chaos that enveloped that fateful day. As the twin towers fell, so too did the illusion of safety that many Americans had held dear. But as the dust settled, a more sinister narrative emerged—one that suggested the government had not only failed to protect its citizens but had actively played a role in orchestrating the events.

The author scrutinized the actions of key political figures, drawing attention to the Project for the New American Century, a neoconservative think tank that had long advocated for military intervention in the Middle East. They highlighted the chilling statements made by its members, suggesting that the American public would require a "new Pearl Harbor" to galvanize support for their agendas. The author's voice trembled with rage as they recounted how the tragedy was used as a pretext for wars that would devastate nations and enrich a select few.

The narrative turned intense as the author detailed the National Security Agency's expansion of surveillance in the wake of 9/11. The Patriot Act, a legislative response to the attacks, eroded civil liberties under the guise of national security. This was a calculated move, the author argued, designed not only to control the narrative but to instill a pervasive fear that would keep the populace compliant and subdued.A Systematic Approach to Control

Through these historical events, the author painted a bleak picture of a government that had systematically crafted a blueprint for control. Each maneuver, each calculated risk, served to fortify its grasp on power. The past was not merely a collection of mistakes; it was a series of strategic moves designed to maintain and expand authority.The author's voice became a rallying cry, urging readers to recognize the patterns that had emerged throughout history. The manipulation of the media, the crafting of public opinion, the exploitation of fear—these were the tools wielded by those in power to maintain their dominance. The unsettling realization that the American system was not as democratic as it seemed loomed heavily over the narrative, forcing readers to grapple with the possibility that their freedoms were an illusion, carefully curated by those who sought to control them.The Shadows of Deception As the chapter drew to a close, the author urged readers to look beyond the surface of the events they had been taught to accept as truth. The shadows of deception lingered over every historical milestone, revealing a disturbing pattern of manipulation. The chilling conclusion was unavoidable: the blueprint of control was not a relic of the past but an ongoing strategy employed to maintain power in the present.

The urgency in the author's words echoed in the silence that followed. The narrative was not just a recounting of history but a call to arms—a plea for awareness in a world where the truth was often obscured by smoke and mirrors. The author's voice lingered in the air, a haunting reminder that the fight for freedom was far from over. The blueprint of control had been drawn, but it was up to the citizens to challenge its authority, to reclaim their agency, and to demand the truth that had been so carefully hidden from them.

As the last flicker of the bulb illuminated the room, the author leaned back, a steely resolve etched on their face. The fight against manipulation and control was just beginning, and they were determined to be at the forefront of a movement that sought to awaken the masses from their complacency. The blueprint had been unveiled, and it was time to dismantle it piece by piece

Chapter 3: Mind Control and Manipulation

The hum of fluorescent lights flickered overhead, casting a sterile glow on the cold, gray walls of the research facility. A sense of unease permeated the air, thick as the clouds that often hovered over the city, shrouding it in a perpetual state of grayness. This was not merely a building; it was a monument to human curiosity, a temple where ethics were sacrificed upon the altar of discovery. This was the heart of MKUltra.

As I delved into the archives, papers scattered across the table, I could almost hear the whispers of the past, echoing the tortured cries of those who had been subjects in this dark experiment. The documents lay open before me like a Pandora's box, ready to unleash the horrors of a clandestine operation that sought to manipulate the very fabric of human consciousness.

The MKUltra program, shrouded in secrecy and conspiracy, was a government initiative that aimed to explore the limits of mind control. It was birthed in the early days of the Cold War, a desperate response to the perceived threat of Soviet influence. The notion was simple: if the enemy could manipulate thoughts, then surely the United States could do the same. But the implementation was anything but simple.

In the neon-lit haze of the 1960s, when the counterculture movement was blooming, the government turned its attention to its own citizens. Young, vibrant, and questioning authority, these individuals became unwitting guinea pigs in a series of experiments that would leave lasting scars on both their minds and society at large. They were told they were part of a groundbreaking study, a noble cause in the name of science. In reality, they were nothing more than pawns in a game played by those in power.

Among the victims was a woman named Susan, a college student whose idealism was as vibrant as her red hair. She had been drawn to the promise of enlightenment through psychedelics, a part of the burgeoning movement that sought to explore the mind's potential. Instead, she found herself trapped in a nightmare.

In her testimony, she recounted the chilling details of her experience: "I was taken into a sterile room, a clinical space that felt more like a prison than a sanctuary for exploration. They administered drugs, substances that twisted my perception of reality, making me question everything I thought I knew. I became a puppet, my thoughts and actions no longer my own."

As I read her words, a chill ran down my spine. The very idea that the government could reduce a person to a mere subject, stripping away their autonomy, was both disturbing and eye-opening. The documents detailed how subjects like Susan were subjected to not only drugs but also psychological torture, all in the name of research. Declassified files revealed a systematic approach to breaking down individuals, mapping their responses like a cartographer charting uncharted territories.

The testimonies of whistleblowers added another layer to the horror. One such individual, Dr. James Miller, a former CIA operative turned informant, had witnessed the program from the inside. His face, lined with age and regret, told a story of complicity and awakening. He spoke passionately about the moral decay that permeated the agency: "We believed we were securing our nation, but in reality, we were dismantling the very freedoms we claimed to protect. The line between patriotism and tyranny blurred before our eyes."

Dr. Miller's words were a stark reminder that the architects of these experiments were not faceless entities. They were individuals, men and women dressed in the armor of authority, wielding power over lives with little regard for the consequences. The chilling realization that they operated in the shadows, guided by a misguided sense of duty, made me question the very fabric of the society we inhabited.

As I continued to sift through the papers, I stumbled upon a particularly haunting report—an internal memo discussing the efficacy of various drugs used in mind control experiments. The language was clinical, devoid of empathy, as if the subjects were mere data points rather than human beings. The memo concluded with a chilling statement: "Further testing required to achieve optimal results."

The implications of these findings were staggering. The government had experimented not only on the vulnerable but had also sought to normalize the idea of manipulation. This was not just about individual lives; it was a commentary on the nature of power itself. How far could one go in the name of control before crossing an irreparable line?

With each revelation, I felt the weight of responsibility pressing down on me. The past was not merely a collection of memories; it was a living entity, pulsating with the pain and suffering of those who had been silenced. The stories of the victims echoed in my mind, a chorus of voices that demanded to be heard.

The tone of the documents shifted as I moved deeper into the research. The initial excitement of exploration gave way to a grim acknowledgment of the program's darker turn. Reports of adverse effects on subjects began to appear with alarming frequency. Some suffered permanent psychological damage, while others simply vanished from the records, their fates sealed in an unmarked grave.

The stories of John, a veteran who had volunteered for the program believing it would assist in his recovery from trauma, broke my heart. He had returned home, a shell of the man who had left. His experiences became a tapestry of torment, woven with threads of paranoia, anxiety, and depressoon he eventually took his own life.

elites, operating in the shadows, will control all the wealth and power. They will have the ability to decide who gets to rise, and who gets left behind.And you? You'll be a cog in the machine, or you'll be replaced.

—-

Conclusion: Breaking Free or Becoming ObsoleteWhat we're witnessing is not an evolution—it's a revolution. A silent one, but a revolution nonetheless. The future of money isn't just digital, it's completely programmable. It's an algorithm, one that decides who gets to succeed and who will stay at the bottom.AI, digital currency, and data aren't just tools. They're the chains that will bind us to a system of control that's impossible to escape. The rich will get richer. The powerful will get more powerful. And the rest of us? We'll be left fighting for crumbs.But it's not too late to fight back. We can expose the game. We can disconnect from the system, seek alternative forms of wealth, and build a life outside the control of these digital overlords. It won't be easy, but it can be done.The question is—are you ready to break free, or are you willing to let this system lock you in.

—-Absolutely. Here's Chapter 10 of The Money Book, aiming for that 2,500-word target. This one dives head-first into debt slavery, how the system traps you from birth, and how every dollar is a chain link unless you learn how to break free.

—-

Chapter 10: Debt by Design – The Invisible Shackles of the Money Machine

Before you take your first breath, you already owe.Before your feet hit the floor, the clock is ticking.And before you understand the value of money, you're already drowning in debt—the most silent and sinister form of slavery ever invented.

In the old days, they used whips and chains.Now ?They use credit scores, interest rates, student loans, and mortgage contracts. And the chains are tighter than ever.

—-

The Origin of Modern Debt Slavery

Let's take it back. Before digital wallets. Before Wall Street. Before the IRS.

The modern debt system was born the moment central banks were allowed to print money out of thin air and charge interest on it.It's the perfect scam:

1. Governments borrow money from central banks.
2. Central banks charge interest on money they never had to begin with.
3. The people—you—are taxed to pay back this imaginary debt.
4. Inflation is triggered to reduce the debt's real value, but your wages stay flat.
5. You borrow to keep up, and boom—you're hooked.

Repeat for 100+ years and you get the modern world: broke, stressed, and begging for crumbs while the top 1% sails yachts made from your dreams.

—-

School: The Indoctrination of Obedience

They didn't teach you how money works.

They taught you how to follow bells, sit still, memorize facts, and obey.

You were trained to clock in, clock out, pay taxes, and stay in your lane. Not to question. Not to build. Not to create generational wealth.

Why didn't they teach compound interest? Inflation? The Federal Reserve scam? The Petrodollar? Budgeting? Taxes? How to start an LLC?Because knowledge breaks chains. And they ain't trying to let you free.

—-

The Birth Certificate Bond

Here's something that'll flip your wig.

Your birth certificate is a financial instrument.The U.S. government registers it, assigns it a number, and then sells bonds based on your future labor to foreign investors and banks.You are collateral.Check your Social Security card—your name is in ALL CAPS. That's your legal fiction, your corporate identity. You are an asset. Your sweat is the yield. Your taxes are the dividends.

They literally bet on your productivity. You've been monetized before you could walk.Still think this is freedom?

—-

Student Loans: The First Trap

Let's say you "do the right thing." Go to college. Get that degree.Welcome to debt for life.Most graduates walk out with $30,000–$100,000+ in loans. Interest compounds. Payments are delayed. But the balance keeps growing.Wanna go bankrupt? Cool—but not on student loans. That's the only debt you can't escape.

They make sure of that.College was never about education. It's about putting you on the hamster wheel before you even start your career. Now you're working just to survive. Just to pay off a degree that probably didn't even get you the job you wanted.You got played.

—-

The Credit System: Modern-Day Plantation LogicCredit is a trap dressed in designer clothes.They tell you to build a credit score to be "trustworthy."But here's the hustle:You need to go into debt to prove you can handle money.The better you are at carrying debt, the more they let you borrow.The more you borrow, the more they own you.It's like being rewarded for being a "good slave."Try to operate outside the system—no loans, no credit cards, no debt? Cool. Your score tanks. You're "untrustworthy." You can't rent, can't buy a car, can't get a house.

This ain't freedom. It's financial apartheid.

—-

Mortgages: Renting from the Bank

"Buy a house," they said. "It's the American dream," they said.

But who really owns that house?

The bank. Until you've paid them back for 15, 30, even 40 years—with interest double what the house is worth.

Miss a few payments?Gone.Foreclosed.

Even if you've paid for 20 years, they'll snatch it like you were just squatting.

So you're not a homeowner. You're a rent-to-own tenant in a bank-owned nation.

—-

Medical Debt: The Cost of Survival

In America, getting sick is a financial crime.Break a leg? That'll be $15,000.

Need surgery? $100k+.And if you don't have insurance? Pray.Medical bankruptcy is the #1 reason Americans file for financial ruin. You can literally die from being too broke to live.Other countries treat healthcare like a human right.

Here? It's just another debt-generating machine for Big Pharma and health insurers.

—-

Inflation: The Hidden Tax

You make more, but your dollar buys less.

That's inflation. But the real kicker?

It's not natural. It's manipulated.

Every time the Fed prints new money, your existing money becomes worthless. Your purchasing power drops. Groceries get more expensive. Gas goes up. Rent rises.

But your wages?Flat.So you work more for less. You grind harder to maintain the same life. And they have the audacity to call that "growth."

—-

Generational Debt: Chains Passed Down

The trap doesn't stop with you.You pass it to your kids.They inherit your student loans, your bad credit, your lack of financial literacy.They start where you left off—in a hole.Meanwhile, rich families pass down trust funds, assets, businesses, property, stocks, connections.They build while we survive.And the cycle continues.

Unless you break it.

—-

Who Benefits From This System?

Follow the money.Every loan you take? Interest goes to a private bank.

Every tax dollar you pay? Part of it pays interest on the national debt—money we shouldn't owe to begin with.

Every inflation bump? That's a wealth transfer from the poor to the rich, from savers to shareholders.

The beneficiaries are always the same:

Central banks Big banks Wall Street

Credit agencies Government contractors

The global eliteYou? You just feed the beast.

—-

How Do You Break Free?

You can't play the game fair and expect to win when it's rigged.But you can opt out, build wealth, and fight back.

Here's how:

1. Learn the Game

Financial literacy is the first weapon. Understand how the system works so you don't get played. Read books. Watch lectures. Study how money, banking, and debt function. Teach your kids.

2. Own Assets, Not Liabilities

Buy income-producing assets: real estate (wisely), businesses, dividend stocks, gold, crypto, intellectual property. Stop buying things that lose value.

3. Use Debt Strategically

There's good debt and bad debt. Good debt builds wealth (e.g., using loans to start a business or buy real estate). Bad debt funds your ego (credit cards, cars, etc.).

4. Start a Side Hustle

Job security is a lie. Multiple income streams are survival. Use your skills. Monetize your knowledge. Build something that no one can take.

5. Pay Yourself First

Save and invest before you pay bills. Automate your wealth building. Even $10 a week grows.

6. Live Below Your Means

Flexing keeps you broke. Freedom lives in frugality.

7. Get Out of Consumer Culture

You don't need new Jordans. You need generational wealth. You don't need a Benz. You need passive income.

—-

This System Only Works If You Obey

Debt slavery is only effective if you keep chasing shiny things and ignore the bars around you.They want you:Distracted by drama.Addicted to dopamine.Insecure about status.Focused on image, not freedom.But you're waking up.

And once you see the game for what it is, you can't unsee it.You can build a new path. Not just for you—but for your bloodline.Break the chain.Reclaim your mind.Own your time.Control your money.

Or someone else will.

—-

Conclusion: The Exit Plan

Debt ain't just numbers. It's a spiritual weight. A mental prison. A generational curse.But every system has a crack.

Every matrix has an exit.And every one of us has the power to say:"I'm done being owned.

The next chapter?

Ownership.Real wealth.And freedom.

Let's go

Chapter 11: Ownership Over Everything – The Real Wealth Formula

You've been told all your life that success is a paycheck, a promotion, a car that turns heads, or a house with a mortgage that'll outlive you.

But here's the truth they don't print in textbooks:Ownership is the new flex.

Not designer clothes. Not leased Benzes.

Not "look rich" vibes. OWN rich.

This chapter ain't about clout. It's about control.

And whoever owns the asset, owns the outcome.

—-

The System Keeps You Renting—On Purpose They want you forever leasing:

Renting your home.Leasing your car.

Subscribing to services.Working someone else's dream.Depending on systems that harvest your time and energy.

They don't want you owning land.

They don't want you owning your name, your content, your business, or even your identity.Why?Because ownership equals power.And power in the wrong hands—meaning yours—is a threat to the status quo.

—-

The Ownership Mindset

Owning ain't just about having stuff. It's a state of mind.It means:

You control your income.

You decide how your time is spent.
You benefit from your labor.
You leave something behind when you die.

It's the opposite of consumption culture.

Instead of flexing for likes, you build for legacy.Let's break it down:

—-

1. Own Your Time

Your 9–5? That's time for sale.

If you don't own your time, you're still a slave—just dressed better, sipping lattes.

Time freedom is the highest form of wealth. If you wake up when you want, move how you want, and earn while you sleep—you won.Build that life. Don't just dream it.

—-

2. Own Your Mind

Don't let the system think for you.

Own your mindset. Own your habits. Own your attention. Because if they control your thoughts, they control your actions—and your money follows your actions.

Read. Question. Unlearn. Reprogram.

—-

3. Own Assets, Not Liabilities

Assets pay you.Liabilities drain you.Simple math.Own what makes you money while you sleep:Rental propertyA digital product

Dividend-paying stocksRoyalties

Intellectual property A brand The goal? Let your money work harder than you do.

—-

4. Own Your Hustle

Don't just get a job—create one.

Your skills can be monetized. Your story, your pain, your experience—that's value.

Turn what you know into a service, a product, a course, a book, a business.

Own the brand.

Own the website.

Own the domain name.

Own the LLC.

Own the customer list.

If you build on someone else's land (Instagram, TikTok, YouTube), they can delete your empire overnight.

So build your own. Digital land is the new real estate.

—-

5. Own Your Network

Relationships = ROI.

The broken network talks about drama and sneakers.The wealth network talks about strategy, capital, and freedom.

Surround yourself with owners. Builders. People who make moves, not excuses.

Ownership rubs off.

—-

6. Own Land

They're not making more land.

Buy a little. Buy a lot. Buy rural. Buy cheap.But own something the system can't replicate or copy-paste.

Because land is one of the last tangible assets that holds real-world value—and when SHTF, owning land means owning leverage.

—-

7. Own Your Story

People out here trying to fit in—nah.

Your story is your brand. Own it.

Your struggles. Your scars. Your survival. It's marketable. It's motivational. It's monetizable.Tell it before they twist it. Publish your own narrative.

Own your voice. The algorithm is always listening—but your truth is louder.

—-

8. Own Equity, Not Just Income

Working for a check is cute. But working for equity? That's freedom.Equity = ownership in a business. Whether it's yours or someone else's, equity means long-term gain over short-term crumbs.

Start a business and grow it.Invest in a friend's startup.Buy stock in companies that print cash.Equity is how the rich get richer. Period.

—-

9. Own Your Digital Self

AI is cloning voices, faces, writing styles.

Data is being sold like hotcakes.

If you're not careful, the system will own your identity too.So protect it:

Own your trademarks.

Own your copyrights.

Own your online presence.

Own your personal brand before someone else does.You're a business. Start acting like it.

—-

10. Own Your Exit Plan

Every owner has an exit.

Employees hope to retire. Owners build exits:

Passive income

Business sales

Licensing deals

Asset liquidation

Trusts and wills

You're not just working for yourself—you're building something that outlives you.

That's the move.

—-

From Ownership to Legacy

Here's the cheat code most never learn:

Ownership turns into freedom. Freedom turns into legacy.You don't have to hustle forever. If you own the right stuff—the game flips.Suddenly:Your kids don't start from zero.Your name holds weight.

Your brand feeds generations.

Your existence shifts culture.

That's the kind of wealth they can't tax or take.

—-

Final Words

The system counts on you being a renter, a borrower, a follower.

But this chapter ain't about following.

It's about planting flags.
It's about building empires.
It's about OWNERSHIP OVER EVERYTHING.
Because once you own—you never beg again.

Chapter 12: Building the Ark – How to Opt-Out and Create a Parallel Economy

They built their world on debt, control, and digital chains.But every empire has cracks. Every system has loopholes. And every cage, no matter how sophisticated, can be broken from the inside out.

This chapter isn't about reforming a sinking ship. It's about building the ark. A parallel economy, a network of freedom, a life raft for those who see the storm coming.

Opting out isn't a weakness. It's strategic defiance. It's recognizing that playing by their rules is a losing game and choosing to create your own.The Illusion of Choice: Why the System Needs Your Participation

The matrix thrives on your participation. Every swipe of your card, every click on an ad, every dollar you "invest" in their rigged markets—it feeds the beast.

They offer you a million shiny distractions, a carefully curated illusion of choice, to keep you within their walled garden. Coke or Pepsi? Democrat or Republican? Netflix or Hulu? It's all the same hand feeding you the same slope.True freedom lies outside these pre-packaged options. It lies in building your own alternatives, in creating value that isn't dependent on their systems of control.The Foundations of a Parallel EconomyBuilding a parallel economy isn't about retreating to a mountain cabin and living off the grid (though for some, that's part of it). It's about creating interconnected networks of exchange, value creation, and community support that operate alongside the mainstream, gradually siphoning its power.

Here are the core pillars:

Decentralized Finance (DeFi): Beyond the hype of meme coins lies the revolutionary potential of decentralized finance. Peer-to-peer lending, yield farming, and truly self-custodial crypto assets offer a way to transact, save, and grow wealth outside the reach of central banks and their surveillance. Understand the risks, do your research, but recognize that DeFi is a fundamental building block of financial sovereignty.

Local and Barter Economies: Remember when communities traded goods and services directly? It wasn't just quaint—it was resilient. Start local barter networks. Support farmers' markets. Engage in skill-sharing. Reduce your dependence on the fragile global supply chain and the inflationary pressures of fiat currency. Your skills and your neighbor's needs are valuable assets.

Community-Supported Agriculture (CSA) and Local Food Systems: Food is foundational. Dependence on centralized, industrial agriculture makes you vulnerable. Support local farmers, join a CSA, or even start your own garden. Building local food security strengthens communities and insulates you from the whims of global corporations and potential supply chain disruptions.

Alternative Currencies and Mutual Credit Systems: Beyond government-issued and even decentralized cryptocurrencies, explore mutual credit systems within your community. These are essentially interest-free IOUs that circulate within a trusted network, facilitating trade without the need for traditional money. They foster local exchange and build community bonds.

Skill-Sharing Networks and Cooperatives: The gig economy isolates. The parallel economy connects. Create skill-sharing networks where members can teach and learn from each other. Form cooperatives for purchasing, production, or housing. Collective action builds resilience and distributes power.

Decentralized Education and Information Networks: Don't rely solely on state-controlled or corporate-sponsored education. Seek out alternative learning resources, independent thinkers, and build your own knowledge base. Support decentralized platforms for sharing information and skills, fostering critical thinking and self-reliance.

Privacy-Focused Technologies and Communication: In a world of increasing surveillance, privacy is paramount. Embrace privacy-focused communication tools, explore decentralized social media alternatives, and learn how to protect your digital footprint. Anonymity can be a form of defense in a system that seeks to track and control every aspect of your life.

Building Your Personal Ark: Practical Steps to Opt-Out

Opting out isn't an overnight revolution. It's a gradual process of shifting your resources, your energy, and your mindset towards greater autonomy. Here are some actionable steps you can take:

Reduce Your Dependence on Mainstream Banks: Explore credit unions, local banks with ethical practices, or the careful use of self-custodial crypto for savings and transactions. Understand the risks and limitations of each, but actively seek alternatives to the big financial institutions.

Prioritize Local and Independent Businesses: Consciously choose to support small businesses in your community over large corporations. This keeps money circulating locally, strengthens your community, and reduces your reliance on globalized systems.

Cultivate Real-World Relationships and Community: The digital world can be isolating. Invest time and energy in building strong relationships with people in your physical community. These connections will be invaluable in times of crisis and for building mutual support networks.

Develop Tangible Skills: In a world increasingly reliant on digital infrastructure, tangible skills become a form of wealth and resilience. Learn to garden, repair things, cook from scratch, provide first aid—skills that are valuable regardless of the state of the mainstream economy.

Invest in Tangible Assets: While digital assets have their place, don't neglect tangible assets that hold intrinsic value, such as precious metals, tools, and stored food. These can provide a hedge against inflation and economic instability

Embrace Frugality and Reduce Consumerism: The consumer culture is designed to keep you in debt and dependent. Consciously reduce your consumption, buy less unnecessary stuff, and prioritize experiences and relationships over material possessions

.

Educate Yourself and Your Family: Financial literacy and an understanding of how the system works are crucial for opting out. Educate yourself and your family about alternative economic models, sound money principles, and the importance of self-reliance.

Start Small and Be Consistent: You don't have to go full off-grid overnight. Start with small, manageable steps and gradually increase your involvement in parallel systems. Consistency is key to building long-term resilience.The Power of Networked IndependenceThe parallel economy isn't about individual isolation; it's about networked independence. It's about building a web of interconnected individuals, families, and communities who are less reliant on the failing mainstream system and more capable of supporting each other.Think of it like a decentralized network, where the strength of the whole comes from the resilience of each individual node. The more people who actively participate in building this parallel world, the stronger and more resilient it becomes.Pushback and Resistance: Navigating the System's Defenses

The architects of the current system won't surrender their control easily. Expect pushback, regulations, and attempts to co-opt or suppress the growth of parallel economies.This is why it's crucial to operate with awareness, to prioritize privacy where necessary, and to build these alternatives with a long-term perspective. Education, community organizing, and peaceful resistance to unjust policies will be essential.

The Moral Imperative: Building a More Just and Sustainable Future

Opting out isn't just about self-preservation; it's about building a more just and sustainable future. The current system is inherently unsustainable, based on endless growth, debt, and the exploitation of both people and the planet.

By creating parallel economies rooted in community, sustainability, and ethical principles, we can lay the foundation for a more resilient and equitable world for ourselves and future generations.

Conclusion: The Seeds of a New World

The digital trap is being laid, but the human spirit's yearning for freedom cannot be contained. By understanding the mechanisms of control and actively building alternatives, we can sow the seeds of a new world—one based on ownership, community, and genuine prosperity.

The ark is under construction. Every act of opting out, every connection forged in the parallel economy, is another plank in its hull. The time to build is now. The future of freedom depends on it.

Chapter 13: The Decentralization Revolution

Blockchain, DAOs, and the Fight for Digital SovereigntyThey centralized everything. Power. Money. Information. Control.

But the internet, born from a spirit of open architecture and peer-to-peer connection, holds the seeds of a powerful counter-movement: decentralization.

Blockchain technology, the engine behind cryptocurrencies, is more than just digital money. It's a paradigm shift. A way to build systems that are transparent, immutable, and free from the control of any single entity.

This chapter is about reclaiming digital sovereignty. About understanding the tools that can dismantle the centralized fortresses and empower individuals with true ownership and control in the digital age.

The Centralization Problem: A Single Point of Failure For centuries, power has consolidated. Kingdoms became nations. Local businesses become multinational corporations. Information flowed through centralized media. Financial power resided in the hands of a few powerful banks.

The digital age initially amplified this trend. Big Tech companies became gatekeepers of information and communication. Central banks extended their reach through digital currencies. Governments increased their surveillance capabilities in the digital realm.

The problem with centralization is its inherent fragility and susceptibility to corruption. A single point of failure can bring down the entire system. A few powerful actors can manipulate the rules for their own benefit. And the masses become increasingly dependent on these centralized authorities.

Blockchain: The Foundation of Trustless Systems

Enter blockchain. At its core, a blockchain is a distributed, immutable ledger. Imagine a shared digital spreadsheet that is constantly updated and verified by a network of computers. Once a transaction is recorded on the blockchain, it cannot be altered or deleted.

This simple yet revolutionary concept enables the creation of trustless systems. You don't need to rely on a central authority (like a bank or a government) to verify transactions or maintain records. The network itself provides security and transparency.

Key characteristics of blockchain technology: Decentralized: No single entity controls the network. Power is distributed among many participants.

Immutable: Once data is recorded, it cannot be changed. This ensures transparency and prevents fraud.

Transparent: All transactions are typically publicly viewable on the blockchain (though the identities of the participants can be pseudonymous).

Secure: Cryptographic hashing and consensus mechanisms ensure the integrity of the data.

Beyond Bitcoin: The Expanding Universe of Blockchain Applications

While Bitcoin was the first and most famous application of blockchain, the technology's potential extends far beyond digital currency. Here are just a few examples:

Smart Contracts: Self-executing contracts with the terms of the agreement directly written into code. They automate processes and eliminate the need for intermediaries in various transactions, from real estate to insurance.

Decentralized Autonomous Organizations (DAOs): Internet-native organizations governed by rules encoded on a blockchain and executed automatically. DAOs allow for collective decision-making and community-driven projects without traditional hierarchical structures.

Supply Chain Management: Blockchain can provide transparent and auditable records of the movement of goods, ensuring authenticity and preventing counterfeiting.

Digital Identity: Self-sovereign identity solutions built on blockchain allow individuals to control their own digital credentials without relying on centralized authorities.

Voting Systems: Blockchain-based voting systems can offer greater transparency and security, potentially increasing trust in democratic processes.

Decentralized Storage: Platforms that utilize blockchain to create distributed networks for storing data, offering an alternative to centralized cloud storage providers.Decentralized Autonomous Organizations (DAOs): The Future of Collective Action?DAOs represent a radical new form of organization. Imagine a company or a community where decisions aren't made by a CEO or a board of directors, but by the collective vote of its members, facilitated by smart contracts on a blockchain.DAOs offer the potential for: Increased Transparency: All rules and transactions are recorded on the blockchain, making them publicly auditable.

Community Governance: Power is distributed among token holders, allowing for more democratic decision-making.

Automation: Smart contracts automatically execute decisions based on the rules encoded in the DAO.

Global Collaboration: DAOs can bring together individuals from anywhere in the world around a common goal.

While DAOs are still in their early stages of development and face challenges related to security and governance, they represent a powerful model for building decentralized communities and organizations that are resistant to censorship and single points of control.

The Fight for Digital Sovereignty: Owning Your Data and Your Identity

In the centralized digital world, your data is not truly yours. It's collected, analyzed, and monetized by large corporations. Your digital identity is often tied to centralized platforms that can censor or restrict your access.

Decentralized technologies offer a path towards digital sovereignty—the ability for individuals to own and control their own data and digital identity.

Self-Sovereign Identity (SSI): Blockchain-based SSI solutions empower individuals to create and manage their own digital credentials, which can be selectively shared with others without relying on central authorities.

Decentralized Social Media: Platforms built on blockchain aim to give users more control over their content and data, offering alternatives to censorship-prone centralized social media giants.

Personal Data Sovereignty: Tools and platforms are emerging that allow individuals to encrypt, store, and control access to their personal data, giving them agency over how it is used.

The fight for digital sovereignty is a fight for fundamental rights in the digital age. Decentralized technologies provide the tools to take back control of our data and our identities.Navigating the Challenges and Risks of Decentralization

While the potential of decentralization is immense, it's important to acknowledge the challenges and risks:

Complexity: Understanding and using decentralized technologies can be technically challenging for the average user.

Security Vulnerabilities: While blockchain itself is secure, applications built on top of it (like smart contracts and DeFi platforms) can have vulnerabilities that can be exploited.

Scalability Issues: Some blockchain networks face challenges in processing a high volume of transactions quickly and efficiently.

Regulatory Uncertainty: Governments around the world are still grappling with how to regulate decentralized technologies, leading to uncertainty and potential restrictions.

Responsibility and Self-Custody: With decentralization comes greater responsibility. Users are responsible for securing their own digital assets and managing their own data.

Despite these challenges, the momentum behind decentralization is undeniable. As the technology matures and becomes more user-friendly, its impact on finance, governance, and individual freedom is likely to grow significantly.

Building the Bridges to a Decentralized Future The transition from a centralized to a decentralized world won't happen overnight. It requires building bridges—user-friendly interfaces, secure infrastructure, and educational resources that empower individuals to participate in these new systems.It also requires a shift in mindset—from relying on centralized authorities to embracing self-sovereignty and community-driven solutions.

Conclusion: The Power to Build a More Open World Decentralized technologies, spearheaded by blockchain, offer a powerful antidote to the dangers of centralized control in the digital age. They provide the tools to build more transparent, secure, and equitable systems for finance, governance, and information sharing.

The revolution is not just about code; it's about empowering individuals with true digital ownership and sovereignty. It's about building a more open and resilient world, one decentralized block at a time.

The power to build this future is in our hands. It's time to learn, to experiment, and to actively participate in the decentralization revolution.

Alright, let's dive into Chapter 14 of The Money Book, focusing on the critical importance of financial education, not just as a means of personal enrichment, but as a fundamental tool for breaking free from the system's control.

Chapter 14: Financial Fortress – The Unbreakable Shield of Education

They keep you financially illiterate for a reason.Confused about credit scores? Intimidated by investing? Overwhelmed by taxes? That's by design.A financially ignorant population is easier to control, easier to exploit, and more dependent on the very systems that are designed to keep them in debt.This chapter is your curriculum. Your guide to building an unbreakable financial fortress through the power of knowledge. Because in the war for your wealth and your freedom, financial education is your most potent weapon.

The Deliberate Obfuscation: Why Financial Literacy Isn't Taught-Think about it. You spend years in school learning algebra, history, and literature. But where are the mandatory courses on budgeting, investing, understanding debt, or navigating the tax system?

The absence is deafening.

The current financial system thrives on complexity and opacity. The more confused you are, the more likely you are to rely on "experts" (who often have their own agendas) and the more vulnerable you are to predatory financial products and services.

They want you to be a consumer, not a builder. A borrower, not a saver. A pawn in their game, not a player. And financial illiteracy is the key to maintaining that power dynamic.Beyond the Basics: What True Financial Education Entails

True financial education goes far beyond simply balancing a checkbook (though that's a good start). It encompasses a deep understanding of:

How Money Works: The history of money, the role of central banks, the mechanics of inflation, and the fundamentals of economic cycles.

Debt and Credit: Understanding different types of debt, the true cost of borrowing, how credit scores are calculated (and manipulated), and strategies for becoming debt-free.

investing: Different asset classes (stocks, bonds, real estate, crypto, precious metals), risk management, diversification, and long-term wealth-building strategies.

Taxes: How the tax system works, legal strategies for minimizing your tax burden, and understanding the implications of different financial decisions on your tax liability.

Entrepreneurship and Business: The fundamentals of starting and running a business, generating multiple income streams, and building scalable enterprises.

Financial Psychology: Understanding your own biases and emotional triggers related to money, and developing a healthy financial mindset.

The Broader Economic and Political Landscape: Recognizing how government policies, global events, and technological advancements impact your financial well-being.

It's a holistic education that empowers you to make informed decisions and take control of your financial future.

Taking Control of Your Financial Education: Resources and Strategies

The good news is that in the age of information, the resources for financial education are abundant—if you know where to look and are willing to put in the work.

Books: There's a wealth of classic and contemporary books on personal finance, investing, and entrepreneurship. Start with the fundamentals and gradually delve into more advanced topics.

Online Courses and Platforms: Numerous online platforms offer courses on everything from budgeting to advanced investment strategies. Seek out reputable sources with a track record of providing unbiased information.

Podcasts and YouTube Channels: Many knowledgeable individuals share valuable financial insights through podcasts and YouTube channels. Look for creators who prioritize education over hype.

Mentors and Communities: Connect with individuals who have achieved financial success and are willing to share their knowledge. Join online or in-person communities focused on financial growth and learning.

Real-World Experience: Don't just learn in theory. Start implementing what you learn in your own life, even if it's with small steps. Open a brokerage account, start a side hustle, track your expenses diligently.

Challenge the Narrative: Be critical of the mainstream financial advice you hear in the media. Understand that many financial institutions have a vested interest in keeping you in their system.

Focus on First Principles: Understand the fundamental principles of wealth building rather than chasing the latest trends or get-rich-quick schemes.

The Power of Compound Knowledge: A Long-Term Investment

Just like compound interest can exponentially grow your wealth over time, compound knowledge can exponentially increase your financial acumen and your ability to make sound decisions.

Every book you read, every course you take, every financial concept you understand builds upon the previous knowledge, creating a powerful foundation for long-term financial success and independence.Think of it as building your financial fortress brick by brick. The stronger your foundation of knowledge, the more resilient you will be to economic storms and the manipulations of the system Financial Education as an Act of DefianceIn a system that profits from your financial ignorance, seeking knowledge is an act of defiance. It's taking back control of your own mind and your own money.

When you understand how the game is played, you can choose not to participate in the ways that keep you trapped. You can make informed decisions about debt, savings, and investments that align with your long-term goals, not the short-term profits of financial institutions.

Financial education empowers you to:

Avoid Predatory Debt: Recognize and steer clear of high-interest loans and other financial traps.

Make Informed Investment Decisions: Grow your wealth strategically rather than gambling on speculation.

Minimize Your Tax Burden: Understand the tax system and legally reduce what you owe.

Build Financial Security: Create a buffer against unexpected expenses and economic downturns.

Pursue Entrepreneurial Opportunities: Develop the financial literacy needed to start and grow a successful business.

Leave a Legacy: Build wealth that can be passed onto future generations.

Teaching the Next Generation: Breaking the Cycle Financial illiteracy is often a generational curse. Children grow up mirroring the financial habits (and often the financial struggles) of their parents.

Breaking this cycle requires actively teaching the next generation about money from a young age. Talk to your kids about budgeting, saving, and the difference between needs and wants. Involve them in financial decisions appropriate for their age. The gift of financial literacy is one of the most valuable inheritances you can provide.

Beyond Personal Gain: The Societal Impact of Financial Literacy

Widespread financial literacy isn't just about individual wealth building; it has broader societal benefits:

* Reduced Inequality: Empowering individuals with financial knowledge can help close the wealth gap.

Stronger Communities: Financially stable individuals are better able to contribute to their communities.

Greater Economic Stability: A more financially literate population is less susceptible to economic shocks and financial crises.

Increased Civic Engagement: When people are not burdened by financial stress, they have more time and energy to engage in civic life.By prioritizing financial education, we can build a more resilient, equitable, and prosperous society for all.

Conclusion: Arm Yourself with Knowledge

The financial landscape is a battlefield, and ignorance is a fatal vulnerability. But knowledge is your armor, your shield, and your most powerful weapon.

Commit to lifelong financial learning. Seek out reliable information. Challenge the status quo. And empower yourself and your loved ones with the understanding needed to build a true financial fortress—one that cannot be easily breached by the forces that seek to control your economic destiny.The journey to financial freedom begins with education. Take the first step, and never stop learning.

Chapter 15: The Double-Edged Sword

–Mastering Strategic Debt for Wealth AccelerationDebt. It's a word that carries a heavy weight, often associated with burden, stress, and the chains of financial servitude, as we explored in Chapter 10. And for good reason – for most, debt is a trap meticulously designed to extract wealth and maintain control.

However, like a double-edged sword, debt, when wielded strategically and with profound understanding, can become a powerful tool for wealth acceleration. The key lies in discerning between good debt and bad debt, and in mastering the principles that allow you to leverage borrowing for exponential growth rather than crippling liability.This chapter isn't about glorifying debt. It's about dissecting it, understanding its nuances, and learning how a select few use it to their advantage to build empires while the masses drown.

The Dichotomy of Debt: Good vs. Bad

The first and most critical step in mastering strategic debt is understanding the fundamental difference between liabilities that drain your wealth and assets that generate it, often financed through debt.

Bad Debt: This is the debt that most people are burdened with. It includes:

High-Interest Consumer Debt: Credit card balances, payday loans, personal loans for non-essential items. This type of debt carries exorbitant interest rates that erode your capital rapidly. It funds consumption, not creation.

Depreciating Asset Loans: Car loans for vehicles that lose value over time. While transportation is often necessary, understanding the true cost of ownership, including interest, depreciation, and insurance, is crucial.

Lifestyle Debt: Borrowing to maintain a lifestyle you can't truly afford. This creates a vicious cycle of working to pay for past consumption rather than investing in your future.Bad debt is a wealth killer. It's a hole in your financial boat that constantly needs patching.Good Debt (Strategic Debt): This is debt used to acquire assets that have the potential to appreciate in value or generate income that exceeds the cost of borrowing. Examples include:

Investment Property Mortgages: Leveraging debt to acquire real estate that generates rental income and appreciates over time. The key here is ensuring the cash flow from the property covers the mortgage payments, property taxes, insurance, and maintenance, ideally with a surplus.Business Loans for Scalable Ventures: Borrowing capital to start or expand a business with a strong potential for profitability and growth. The return on investment from the business should far outweigh the interest paid on the loan.

Margin Loans for Income-Generating Assets (Advanced): A more sophisticated and higher-risk strategy involving borrowing against existing investments to purchase more assets. This requires a deep understanding of market dynamics and risk management.Good debt, when managed prudently, acts as leverage, amplifying your returns and accelerating your wealth-building trajectory.The Principles of Strategic Debt Utilization

Simply taking on debt for an asset doesn't automatically make it "good debt." The strategy lies in the execution. Here are key principles to consider:Positive Cash Flow: The asset acquired through debt should generate income that exceeds the total cost of the debt (interest and principal payments) and associated expenses. If your rental property consistently costs you more than it brings in, it's not strategic debt, it's a liability disguised as an asset.

Appreciation Potential: The asset should have a reasonable expectation of increasing in value over time. Real estate in growing areas, well-chosen businesses with strong growth potential, and certain other asset classes can offer this appreciation.

Tax Advantages: In many jurisdictions, interest paid on certain types of debt (like mortgages on investment properties or business loans) can be tax-deductible, further enhancing the returns. Understanding and utilizing these tax benefits is a crucial part of strategic debt management. Controlled Risk: While leverage can amplify gains, it also amplifies losses. Thorough due diligence, conservative loan-to-value ratios, and robust risk management strategies are essential. Avoid over-leveraging to the point where a minor market fluctuation could lead to financial ruin.Exit Strategy: Always have a clear plan for how and when you will eventually pay off the debt or realize the gains from the asset. This could involve selling the asset, refinancing, or the asset generating enough passive income to cover the debt entirely

Understanding the Terms: Meticulously review and understand the terms of any loan agreement, including interest rates (fixed vs. variable), repayment schedules, fees, and any potential penalties.

Case Studies in Strategic Debt

Consider these examples to illustrate the power of strategic debt:

The Real Estate Investor: Acquires a multi-family property with a mortgage. The rental income from the tenants covers the mortgage payments, property taxes, insurance, and maintenance, with a positive cash flow. Over time, the property appreciates in value, and the investor builds equity while the tenants essentially pay down the debt.

The Business Owner: Takes out a loan to purchase new equipment that significantly increases production capacity and reduces operating costs. The increased profitability of the business far outweighs the interest payments on the loan, leading to faster growth and higher overall profits.

The Stock Market Investor (Advanced): Carefully uses margin to invest in dividend-paying stocks. The dividend income generated exceeds the interest paid on the margin loan, creating additional income. However, this strategy carries significant risk and requires a deep understanding of market dynamics and risk tolerance.In each of these scenarios, debt is not a burden but a tool used to acquire income-generating or appreciating assets, accelerating the wealth-building process.The Mindset Shift: From Debt Aversion to Strategic LeverageMany people have a deep-seated aversion to debt, often stemming from negative experiences or societal conditioning. While avoiding bad debt is crucial, overcoming the fear of all debt is necessary to unlock its potential as a wealth-building tool.

This requires a significant mindset shift:

Education Over Emotion: Base your debt decisions on logic, analysis, and a thorough understanding of the numbers, rather than fear or emotional impulses.

Long-Term Perspective: Strategic debt is often a long-term game. Focus on the potential for long-term appreciation and income generation rather than short-term gains.Calculated Risk-Taking: Understand and accept that all investment involves risk, and strategic debt amplifies that risk. However, with proper due diligence and risk management, the potential rewards can be substantial. The Dangers of Unstrategic Debt It's crucial to reiterate the dangers of unstrategic debt. Falling into the trap of high-interest consumer debt can derail your financial progress for years, if not decades. The interest paid on bad debt is wealth being siphoned away from your future.The key takeaway is that debt is a tool, and like any tool, it can be used to build or destroy. The determining factor is the knowledge, discipline, and strategic intent of the wielder.

Conclusion: Harnessing the Power of LeverageStrategic debt, when understood and applied correctly, can be a powerful catalyst for wealth acceleration. It allows you to leverage other people's money to acquire assets that generate income and appreciate in value.However, it is a double-edged sword that demands respect, education, and meticulous management. Without a clear understanding of good debt versus bad debt, the principles of strategic utilization, and the inherent risks involved, debt can quickly become a crippling burden.

Mastering strategic debt is about transforming a potential liability into a powerful asset in your wealth-building arsenal. It's about using leverage intelligently to build your financial fortress faster and more efficiently.

Chapter 16: The Untapped Goldmine

–

The single paycheck is a precarious perch. It leaves you vulnerable to layoffs, economic downturns, and the whims of a single employer. It limits your growth potential and keeps you tethered to a system where your time is directly exchanged for a finite amount of money.

True financial freedom and security are rarely built on a single pillar. The wealthy understand the power of diversification, not just in their investments, but also in their income sources. Building multiple streams of income is like constructing a financial safety net with many strong ropes – if one breaks, you don't fall.

This chapter is about unlocking the untapped goldmine of your skills, knowledge, and assets to create a portfolio of income streams that provide stability, accelerate wealth accumulation, and ultimately buy back your time.

Beyond the 9-to-5: Why One Income Stream is a Risk

The traditional employment model, while offering stability for some, inherently carries significant risks:

Single Point of Failure: Losing your job eliminates your entire income overnight, potentially leading to financial crisis.

Limited Growth Potential: Your income is typically capped by your salary and the rate of promotions within a single organization.Time for Money Exchange: Your income is directly tied to the hours you work, limiting your ability to scale your earnings beyond your physical capacity.

Dependence on an Employer: Your financial well-being is dependent on the decisions and performance of an entity outside of your direct control.

Relying solely on a single income stream is like navigating a treacherous sea in a boat with only one sail. Building multiple streams is like adding more sails and even an engine, providing greater stability and the ability to reach your destination faster and more reliably.Unlocking Your Income Potential: Identifying Your Assets

The first step in building multiple income streams is to identify the assets you already possess that can be monetized. These can include:

Skills and Expertise: What are you good at? What knowledge do you have that others would pay for? This could range from writing, coding, design, consulting, teaching, or any specialized skill.

Time: While your 9-to-5 exchanges time for money, can you leverage your spare time to create additional income through side hustles or freelance work?

Capital: Do you have savings or investments that can generate income through dividends, interest, or capital gains?

Physical Assets: Do you own property that can be rented out? Possess items that can be sold or lent?Digital Assets: Can you create digital products like ebooks, courses, templates, or software that can be sold online?

Network and Connections: Can you leverage your relationships to facilitate deals, make referrals, or create partnerships that generate income?

Everyone possesses a unique combination of these assets. The key is to identify them and explore their potential for income generation.Building Your Income Portfolio: Diverse StrategiesOnce you've identified your assets, you can explore various strategies for building multiple income streams: Freelancing and Consulting: Offer your skills and expertise on a project basis to multiple clients. This allows you to leverage your existing knowledge and set your own rates.Creating and Selling Digital Products: Develop ebooks, online courses, software, templates, or other digital assets that can be sold repeatedly with minimal ongoing effort, creating passive or semi-passive income.Affiliate Marketing: Partner with businesses and promote their products or services, earning a commission on each sale generated through your unique referral link.

Investing in Income-Generating Assets: Invest in dividend-paying stocks, bonds, or real estate that provide a regular stream of passive income.Building and Monetizing Online Content: Create a blog, YouTube channel, podcast, or social media presence around a topic you're passionate about and monetize it through advertising, sponsorships, or selling your own products and services.Starting a Side Hustle or Small Business: Leverage your skills or interests to create a part-time business that generates additional income. This could eventually grow into a full-time venture.Peer-to-Peer Lending and Other Alternative Investments: Explore platforms that allow you to lend money to individuals or businesses for interest, or invest in other alternative assets that generate income.Royalties and Licensing: If you create intellectual property like music, art, or inventions, you can earn royalties or licensing fees when others use your work.

The key is to diversify your income sources, just as you would diversify your investment portfolio. This reduces your reliance on any single stream and provides greater financial stability.The Power of Leverage and Automation

As you build multiple income streams, look for opportunities to leverage your time and automate processes. This is where the real magic of income diversification happens.Creating Digital Products: Once created, a digital product can be sold countless times with minimal additional effort. Building Scalable Online Businesses: Online businesses can reach a global audience and often have lower overhead costs than traditional brick-and-mortar ventures.

Utilizing Automation Tools: Tools for email marketing, social media scheduling, and e-commerce can automate many of the repetitive tasks involved in running an online business.Outsourcing: As your income grows, consider outsourcing tasks that you don't enjoy or that are not the best use of your time, freeing you up to focus on higher-value activities.Leverage and automation allow you to decouple your income from your direct time input, creating the potential for exponential growth and greater time freedom.

The Mindset of Abundance: Moving Beyond Scarcity Building multiple income streams often requires a shift from a mindset of scarcity to a mindset of abundance. This involves believing that there are enough opportunities and resources available for you to create multiple sources of income.It also requires a willingness to experiment, to learn new skills, and to step outside of your comfort zone. Not every income stream you pursue will be successful, but each attempt provides valuable learning experiences and moves you closer to your goals.Managing Multiple Income Streams: Organization and StrategyAs your income streams grow, it's crucial to implement effective organizational and management strategies:Separate Tracking: Keep detailed records of the income and expenses associated with each income stream. Tax Planning: Understand the tax implications of each income source and plan accordingly.

Reinvestment: Strategically reinvest a portion of your earnings to further grow your existing income streams or create new ones. Time Management: Effectively allocate your time and energy across your various income-generating activities.

Treat your income portfolio like a business, with clear goals, strategies, and performance tracking.

Conclusion: Building Your Financial Fortress of Income Building multiple streams of income is not just about making more money; it's about building a more resilient and secure financial future. It's about taking control of your financial destiny and reducing your dependence on a single point of failure.

By identifying your assets, exploring diverse income-generating strategies, leveraging automation, and cultivating a mindset of abundance, you can unlock the untapped goldmine of your potential and build a financial fortress of income streams that provides stability, accelerates wealth accumulation, and ultimately buys back your most valuable asset: your time.

The single paycheck is a starting point, not the destination. The path to true financial freedom lies in building a diversified and robust portfolio of income sources.

Chapter 17: The Art of Defense – Shielding Your Assets

You've worked hard to accumulate wealth, whether through strategic debt utilization, building multiple income streams, or disciplined saving and investing. But the game isn't over once you have assets. In many ways, it's just beginning.

The world is full of predators – from frivolous lawsuits and unexpected creditors to excessive taxation and economic instability. Without a robust defense strategy, your hard-earned wealth can be chipped away, seized, or even completely wiped out.

This chapter is your guide to building an impenetrable financial fortress, not just by accumulating assets, but by strategically shielding them from the various perils that threaten your financial security. The art of defense is just as crucial as the art of offense in the long-term wealth-building game.Identifying the Threats to Your WealthTo effectively protect your assets, you must first understand the potential threats:

Lawsuits: In an increasingly litigious society, anyone can be sued, regardless of fault. Personal injury claims, business disputes, and even frivolous lawsuits can put your assets at risk.Creditors: Unexpected debt, medical bills, or business liabilities can lead creditors to pursue your assets to satisfy those debts.

Taxes: While necessary for funding public services, excessive or poorly planned taxation can significantly erode your wealth over time, especially through estate taxes.

Economic Instability: Inflation, market crashes, and government policies can devalue your assets or limit your access to them.Divorce: In the unfortunate event of divorce, assets accumulated during the marriage are often subject to division.

Estate Planning Neglect: Failing to plan for the transfer of your assets upon death can lead to significant taxes, legal fees, and delays for your heirs.

Scams and Fraud: The digital age has ushered in a new era of sophisticated scams and fraudulent schemes designed to steal your wealth.

Understanding these potential threats is the first step in building an effective asset protection strategy.

The Cornerstones of Asset Protection

Effective asset protection isn't about hiding assets illegally; it's about legally structuring your affairs to minimize risk and maximize the preservation of your wealth. Here are some key cornerstones:

Proper Insurance: Adequate insurance coverage is the first line of defense against many potential liabilities. This includes homeowners insurance, auto insurance, umbrella insurance (providing additional liability coverage), professional liability insurance (if applicable), and health insurance. Ensure your coverage limits are sufficient to protect your net worth.

Strategic Ownership Structures: How you own your assets can significantly impact their vulnerability. Consider using legal entities like Limited Liability Companies (LLCs) for business assets and potentially for real estate to separate personal liability from business or property risks.

rusts: Various types of trusts can offer significant asset protection benefits. Irrevocable trusts, in particular, can shield assets from creditors and estate taxes, as the assets are legally owned by the trust, not the grantor. Spendthrift trusts can protect beneficiaries from their own creditors.

Retirement Accounts: In many jurisdictions, qualified retirement accounts like 401(k)s and IRAs have significant protection from creditors under federal and state laws. Maximize contributions to these accounts as part of your overall asset protection strategy.

* Homestead Exemptions: Many states offer homestead exemptions that protect a certain amount of equity in your primary residence from creditors. Understand the laws in your jurisdiction.

* Prenuptial and Postnuptial Agreements: These legal agreements can define how assets will be divided in the event of divorce, providing clarity and protection for both parties.

* Offshore Asset Protection (Advanced): For high-net-worth individuals, strategically structuring assets in jurisdictions with strong asset protection laws can offer an additional layer of defense. However, this is a complex area requiring expert legal counsel and full compliance with all tax laws.

* Careful Financial Planning: A comprehensive financial plan that considers potential risks and incorporates asset protection strategies is crucial. Work with qualified professionals like estate planning attorneys and financial advisors who specialize in asset protection.

Structuring Ownership for Protection: The Power of Legal Entities

Choosing the right ownership structure for your assets is a fundamental aspect of asset protection.

* Sole Proprietorship/Partnership (Without Protection): Owning assets directly in your name or through a simple sole proprietorship or partnership exposes those assets to personal liability for business debts or lawsuits.

* Limited Liability Company (LLC): An LLC can provide a shield between your personal assets and your business liabilities. If your business is sued, your personal assets (like your home or personal investments) are generally protected. Similarly, your business assets are typically protected from personal lawsuits unrelated to the business.

* Corporations (S-Corp, C-Corp): Corporations also offer liability protection, separating the owners from the debts and obligations of the business. The choice between an S-Corp and a C-Corp often depends on tax considerations.

The key is to understand the liability implications of different ownership structures and choose the ones that best protect your assets based on your specific circumstances.

The Strategic Use of Trusts for Asset Preservation

Trusts are powerful legal tools for asset protection and estate planning.Revocable Trusts (Living Trusts): While primarily used to avoid probate, revocable trusts offer some limited creditor protection in certain jurisdictions. Because the grantor (the person who creates the trust) retains control over the assets, they generally aren't fully protected from the grantor's creditors.

* Irrevocable Trusts: Once established, the grantor typically cannot change or terminate an irrevocable trust. Because the assets are legally owned by the trust and are no longer considered the grantor's property, they can offer significant protection from the grantor's creditors and may also provide estate tax benefits.

* Spendthrift Trusts: These trusts are designed to protect a beneficiary's inheritance from their own creditors or from their own mismanagement. The beneficiary typically cannot directly access the principal and may receive distributions at the trustee's discretion.

Choosing the right type of trust depends on your specific goals, the nature of your assets, and the level of protection you seek.

Navigating the Complexities of Offshore Asset Protection

For individuals with substantial wealth, offshore asset protection trusts and other structures in jurisdictions with favorable laws can offer a significant layer of defense against potential lawsuits and creditors.

However, this is a complex and highly regulated area. It's crucial to:Work with Experienced Legal Counsel: Ensure full compliance with all domestic and international tax laws and reporting requirements.

* Choose Reputable Jurisdictions: Select jurisdictions with a proven track record of strong asset protection laws and a stable legal system.

* Understand the Costs and Complexity: Offshore structures can be expensive to set up and maintain.

Offshore asset protection should only be considered with expert guidance and a thorough understanding of the implications. It is not a tool for hiding assets illegally or evading taxes.

The Importance of Proactive Planning

Asset protection is not something you do when a lawsuit is filed against you; by then, it's often too late. Effective asset protection requires proactive planning and the implementation of strategies before any potential threats arise.

Think of it like building a strong wall around your financial fortress before the invaders arrive. Once the attack begins, it's much harder to erect defenses.

Regularly review your asset protection strategies with your legal and financial advisors to ensure they are still appropriate for your circumstances and comply with any changes in the law.

Ethical Considerations in Asset Protection

While the goal of asset protection is to legally shield your wealth, it's crucial to operate ethically and within the bounds of the law. Asset protection strategies should not be used to fraudulently conceal assets or evade legitimateThe focus should be on legitimate legal structures and strategies designed to minimize risk and preserve wealth for yourself and your heirs in a responsible manner.

Conclusion: Building an Impenetrable Financial Fortress

Protecting your assets is an integral part of long-term financial success. It's about safeguarding the wealth you've accumulated from the various predators and perils that can threaten your financial security.

By understanding the potential threats, implementing sound asset protection strategies like proper insurance, strategic ownership structures, and trusts, and engaging in proactive planning with qualified professionals, you can build an impenetrable financial fortress that will withstand the storms and ensure the preservation of your wealth for generations to come.

The art of defense is not about paranoia; it's about prudence and responsibility in managing the fruits of your labor. It's about ensuring that your hard work benefits you and your loved ones, not those who seek to take it away.

Chapter 18: Leaving Your Legacy

– The Essential Art of Estate Planning

You've built wealth, protected it, and navigated the complexities of the financial world. But the final act of responsible financial stewardship lies in ensuring your assets are transferred according to your wishes and with minimal burden on your loved ones. planning – a process often delayed or avoided, yet absolutely crucial for securing your legacy and providing for those you care about.

Estate planning isn't just for the wealthy. It's for anyone who has assets they want to pass on, anyone who wants to designate guardians for their children, and anyone who wants to spare their family the stress and expense of a potentially complicated probate process. It's the ultimate act of love and responsibility.

Why Estate Planning is Not Just for the Rich

The common misconception is that estate planning is only relevant for the wealthy with sprawling estates. This couldn't be further from the truth. Consider these scenarios:

* Parents with Minor Children: Without a will, the court will decide who becomes the legal guardian of your children, which may not align with your wishes. Estate planning allows you to nominate guardians you trust.

* Individuals with Specific Wishes: If you want certain assets to go to specific individuals or charities, a will ensures your intentions are legally documented and followed.

* Avoiding Probate: Probate is the legal process of validating a will and distributing assets, which can be time-consuming, expensive, and public. Proper estate planning can help your loved ones avoid or streamline this process.

* Minimizing Estate Taxes: While federal estate taxes primarily affect larger estates, state estate taxes can have lower thresholds. Strategic planning can help minimize these burdens.

* Planning for Incapacity: Estate planning documents can also include provisions for who will manage your financial and healthcare decisions if you become incapacitated.

For everyone with assets and loved ones, estate planning provides peace of mind and ensures your wishes are respected.

The Key Components of a Comprehensive Estate Plan

A well-rounded estate plan typically includes several key documents:

* Last Will and Testament (Will): This legal document outlines how you want your assets distributed after your death. It allows you to name beneficiaries, designate an executor to manage your estate, and nominate guardians for minor children. Without a will, your assets will be distributed according to your state's intestacy laws, which may not reflect your desires.

* Revocable Living Trust: This trust is created during your lifetime and allows you to transfer assets into it while still maintaining control as the trustee. Upon your death, the assets in the trust pass directly to your beneficiaries without going through probate, offering privacy and potentially faster distribution. It can also provide for management of your assets if you become incapacitated.

* Irrevocable Trusts: As discussed in Chapter 17, these trusts offer significant asset protection and potential estate tax benefits because the assets are legally owned by the trust and are no longer considered part of your taxable estate.

* Power of Attorney (POA) for Finances: This document designates someone you trust (your agent or attorney-in-fact) to manage your financial affairs if you become unable to do so yourself. There are different types of POAs, including durable POAs that remain in effect even if you become incapacitated.

* Advance Healthcare Directives (Living Will and Healthcare POA): These documents outline your wishes regarding medical treatment if you are unable to communicate them yourself. A living will specify the types of medical care you do or do not want, while a healthcare POA designates someone to make healthcare decisions on your behalf.

* Beneficiary Designations: For certain assets like life insurance policies and retirement accounts, you directly name beneficiaries. These assets typically pass directly to the named beneficiaries outside of your will or trust. It's crucial to keep these designations up to date.

* Letter of Intent: While not legally binding, a letter of intent can provide your executor and loved ones with additional guidance on your wishes, such as funeral arrangements, personal belongings, and values you want to be remembered for.

Navigating the Probate Process: Why Avoidance is Often Key

Probate is the legal process of administering a deceased person's estate. It involves validating the will (if one exists), identifying and valuing assets, paying debts and taxes, and distributing the remaining assets to the beneficiaries.

Probate can be:

* Time-Consuming: It can take months or even years to complete, during which time your assets may be frozen.

* Expensive: Legal fees, executor fees, and court costs can significantly reduce the value of your estate.

* Public Record: Probate proceedings are generally public, meaning your financial affairs become open to scrutiny.

* Stressful for Heirs: The legal complexities and delays can add significant emotional and financial stress to your grieving loved ones.

Proper estate planning, particularly the use of revocable living trusts and careful beneficiary designations, can often help your estate avoid or minimize the probate process, ensuring a smoother and more private transfer of assets to your beneficiaries.

Minimizing Estate Taxes: Strategic Planning for the Future

Estate taxes are levied on the transfer of wealth upon death. While federal estate taxes currently have a high exemption threshold, state estate taxes can apply to smaller estates. Strategic estate planning can help minimize these taxes:

* Gifting Strategies: Making lifetime gifts within the annual exclusion amount can reduce the size of your taxable estate.

* Irrevocable Life Insurance Trusts (ILITs): These trusts can hold life insurance policies outside of your taxable estate, ensuring the death benefit passes to your beneficiaries tax-free.

* Qualified Personal Residence Trusts (QPRTs): These trusts allow you to transfer your home out of your taxable estate while retaining the right to live in it for a specified term.

* Family Limited Partnerships (FLPs) and Limited Liability Companies (LLCs): These entities can be used to transfer business interests and other assets to family members while potentially reducing their taxable value.

Tax laws are complex and subject to change, so it's essential to work with experienced estate planning professionals to develop strategies tailored to your specific situation.

Planning for Incapacity: Protecting Yourself During Your Lifetime

Estate planning isn't just about what happens after death; it also involves planning for potential incapacity during your lifetime. Durable powers of attorney for finances and healthcare directives ensure that if you become unable to manage your own affairs, someone you trust can step in to make decisions on your behalf, protecting your financial well-being and ensuring your healthcare wishes are respected.

The Importance of Regular Review and Updates

Your life circumstances, family situation, and the law can change over time. It's crucial to review and update your estate plan periodically – ideally every 3-5 years, or whenever significant life events occur (marriage, divorce, birth of children, death of a beneficiary, significant changes in assets or the law). An outdated estate plan may not reflect your current wishes or may have unintended consequences.

Choosing the Right Estate Planning Professionals

Navigating the complexities of estate planning requires the expertise of qualified professionals:

* Estate Planning Attorney: An experienced attorney can help you understand the laws in your jurisdiction, draft the necessary legal documents, and ensure your plan is legally sound and achieves your goals.

* Financial Advisor: A financial advisor can help you integrate your estate plan with your overall financial plan, considering tax implications and asset transfer strategies.

* Tax Advisor: A tax advisor can provide guidance on minimizing estate and gift taxes.

Work with professionals you trust and who have a strong understanding of estate planning principles.

Leaving a Legacy Beyond Finances

While estate planning often focuses on the transfer of financial assets, consider also how you want to leave a legacy beyond money. This might include:

* Values and Beliefs: Share your core values and life lessons with your loved ones through letters or video recordings.

* Personal Belongings: Decide who should receive sentimental items and heirlooms.

* Philanthropic Intentions: Incorporate charitable giving into your estate plan.

A comprehensive legacy encompasses not just your wealth, but also your wisdom and your values.

Conclusion: Securing Your Family's Future and Your Peace of Mind

Estate planning is a critical aspect of responsible financial stewardship. It's about ensuring your assets are protected, your loved ones are provided for, and your wishes are honored. While it may seem daunting, the peace of mind that comes from having a well-crafted estate plan in place is invaluable. It's the final, thoughtful act of ensuring your legacy lives on according to your intentions. Don't delay this essential task – secure your family's future and your own peace of mind by engaging in comprehensive estate planning today.

Chapter 19: Decoding the Matrix

–Mastering the Tax System to Protect Your Wealth

Taxes. For many, it's a four-letter word associated with complexity, frustration, and the feeling that a significant portion of their hard-earned income vanishes into a seemingly opaque system. However, understanding the tax system is not just a civic duty; it's a critical element of protecting and growing your wealth.

The tax code, in all its intricate glory (or infamy), contains both obligations and opportunities. Those who navigate it strategically can significantly reduce their tax burden, freeing up more capital for saving, investing, and building their financial future. Those who remain ignorant often overpay, unknowingly subsidizing those who understand the rules of the game.

This chapter is your guide to decoding the tax matrix, understanding its fundamental principles, and implementing legal strategies to minimize your tax liability and keep more of what you earn.

Understanding the Fundamentals: How the Tax System Works

The tax system in most developed nations is a complex web of laws, regulations, and interpretations. However, understanding some basic principles is essential:

* Taxable Income: This is the portion of your income that is subject to taxation after deductions and exemptions.

* Tax Brackets: Income is often taxed at progressive rates, meaning higher levels of income are taxed at higher percentages.

* Deductions: These reduce your taxable income. They can be standard deductions (a fixed amount) or itemized deductions (specific expenses).

* Credits: These directly reduce the amount of tax you owe, offering a dollar-for-dollar reduction.

* Capital Gains Tax: Profits from the sale of assets like stocks or real estate are often taxed at different rates than ordinary income, typically lower for long-term holdings.

* Different Types of Taxes: Income tax is just one form of taxation. Others include payroll taxes (for Social Security and Medicare), sales tax, property tax, and potentially estate and gift taxes.

Grasping these fundamental concepts provides a framework for understanding how your financial decisions impact your tax liability.

Strategic Tax Planning: Minimizing Your Burden Legally

The goal of strategic tax planning is not to evade taxes (which is illegal), but to minimize your tax liability by taking advantage of all legal deductions, credits, and tax-advantaged structures available to you.

* Maximize Retirement Contributions: Contributions to tax-advantaged retirement accounts like 401(k)s, traditional IRAs, and SEP IRAs can be tax-deductible, reducing your current taxable income. Roth accounts offer tax-free growth and withdrawals in retirement.

* Utilize Health Savings Accounts (HSAs): If you have a high-deductible health plan, contributing to an HSA offers a triple tax advantage: contributions are tax-deductible, earnings grow tax-free, and withdrawals for qualified medical expenses are tax-free.

* Claim All Eligible Deductions: Understand the various itemized deductions you may be eligible for, such as mortgage interest, state and local taxes (within limits), charitable contributions, and medical expenses (above a certain threshold). Keep thorough records of potential deductions.

* Take Advantage of Tax Credits: Explore available tax credits, such as those for education expenses, child care, energy efficiency improvements, and certain investments. Credits offer a direct reduction in your tax bill.

* Strategically Manage Capital Gains and Losses: Understand the tax implications of buying and selling investments. Holding assets for the long term (more than a year) typically results in lower capital gains tax rates. Tax-loss harvesting (selling losing investments to offset gains) can also reduce your tax liability.

* Choose Tax-Efficient Investments: Some investments, like municipal bonds, offer tax-exempt interest income. Consider the tax efficiency of different investment vehicles.

* Structure Your Business Wisely: The legal structure of your business (sole proprietorship, LLC, S-Corp, C-Corp) can have significant tax implications. Consult with a tax professional to choose the structure that is most advantageous for your specific situation.

* Plan for Self-Employment Taxes: If you are self-employed, understand that you are responsible for both the employee and employer portions of Social Security and Medicare taxes. Strategically deducting business expenses can help offset this burden.

* Consider Tax-Advantaged Trusts: As discussed in Chapter 18, certain types of trusts can offer estate and gift tax benefits, helping to preserve wealth for future generations.

The Importance of Record Keeping and Organization

Effective tax planning requires meticulous record keeping. Keep detailed records of all income, expenses, and investment transactions. Organize your documents in a way that makes it easy to prepare your tax returns or provide information to a tax professional. Good record keeping will ensure you can accurately claim all eligible deductions and credits.

Understanding Tax Law Changes and Staying Informed

Tax laws are constantly evolving. Stay informed about changes in tax legislation and regulations that may affect your financial situation. Subscribe to reputable financial news sources, follow tax professionals on social media, or consider using tax software that updates with the latest changes.

When to Seek Professional Tax Advice

While understanding the basics is crucial, the tax system can be complex, and individual situations vary. It's often wise to seek professional advice from a qualified tax advisor or CPA, especially when:

* Your financial situation is complex (e.g., you own a business, have significant investments, or have multiple sources of income).

* You are facing significant life events (e.g., marriage, divorce, sale of a business, inheritance).

* You are unsure about specific deductions or credits.

* You want to develop a comprehensive tax planning strategy.

A good tax advisor can help you navigate the complexities of the tax code, identify opportunities for tax savings, and ensure you are in compliance with all regulations.

The Ethical Considerations of Tax Minimization While the goal is to minimize your tax liability legally, it's important to operate ethically and within the spirit of the law. Aggressive tax avoidance schemes can attract scrutiny from tax authorities and potentially lead to penalties. Focus on legitimate strategies and transparency in your tax reporting.Beyond Income Tax: Understanding Other Taxes Don't focus solely on income tax. Be aware of other taxes that can impact your wealth:

Sales Tax: Understand the sales tax rates in your area and how they affect your purchasing decisions.Property Tax: If you own real estate, factor in property taxes as a significant op pop-upngoing expense.Estate and Gift Taxes: As discussed in Chapter 18, plan strategically to minimize these taxes on the transfer of wealth.A holistic understanding of the entire tax landscape is crucial for comprehensive financial planning.Conclusion: Mastering the Tax Code for Financial Empowerment

The tax system doesn't have to be an impenetrable fortress. By understanding its fundamental principles, engaging in strategic tax planning, maintaining meticulous records, and seeking professional advice when needed, you can decode the matrix and significantly reduce your tax burden. This isn't about being unpatriotic; it's about being financially savvy and keeping more of the wealth you've worked hard to earn. Mastering the tax code is a crucial step towards greater financial empowerment and building a more secure financial future. Don't let ignorance cost you – take the time to understand the rules of the game and play it to your advantage.

Chapter 20: Self-Talk:

Replace negative thoughts about money with positive affirmations and beliefs about your ability to create wealth.

Focus on Creation, Not Just Consumption: Shift your energy from simply acquiring things to creating value and generating income.

See Opportunities, Not Obstacles: Reframe challenges as opportunities for learning and growth.Celebrate Others' Success: Avoid envy and instead celebrate the achievements of others, recognizing that their success doesn't diminish your own potentialMastering Fear and Greed: The Emotional Drivers of Financial Mistakes Fear and greed are two of the most powerful emotions that can derail financial decisions. Fear of Missing Out (FOMO): Can lead to impulsive investments in hyped-up assets without proper due diligence. Fear of Loss: Can cause you to sell investments prematurely during market downturns, locking in losses. Greed: Can drive you to take on excessive risk in pursuit of unrealistic returns.Developing emotional intelligence in your financial involves:Self-Awareness: Recognizing your emotional triggers and how they influence your financial decisions. Emotional Regulation: Learning to manage and control your emotional responses to market

– Cultivating the Mindset for Long-Term Financial Success

The mechanics of money – budgeting, investing, tax planning – are crucial. But they are only half the equation. The other, often more significant, half is the inner game: the mindset, beliefs, and emotional intelligence that drive your financial decisions and ultimately determine your long-term success.

You can have all the financial knowledge in the world, but if your mindset is plagued by fear, impulsivity, or a scarcity mentality, your financial journey will be an uphill battle. Cultivating the right mindset is the foundation upon which lasting wealth and financial freedom are built.

This chapter delves into the essential mental frameworks, habits, and emotional skills that separate those who achieve lasting financial success from those who perpetually struggle, regardless of their income level.

Overcoming the Scarcity Mindset: Embracing Abundance

A scarcity mindset is characterized by the belief that there is never enough – enough money, enough opportunities, enough resources. This mindset often leads to fear-based decisions, hoarding, and a reluctance to invest or take calculated risks.

Cultivating an abundance mindset involves recognizing that opportunities are plentiful, and your potential for wealth creation is limitless. This shift in perspective fosters a sense of optimism, encourages proactive behavior, and opens you up to new possibilities for growth.

Strategies for shifting to an abundance mindset: Gratitude: Regularly focus on what you already have and express gratitude for it. This shifts your focus from lack to appreciation.

Positive Self-Talk: Replace negative thoughts about money with positive affirmations and beliefs about your ability to create wealth.

Focus on Creation, Not Just Consumption: Shift your energy from simply acquiring things to creating value and generating income.

See Opportunities, Not Obstacles: Reframe challenges as opportunities for learning and growth.

Celebrate Others' Success: Avoid envy and instead celebrate the achievements of others, recognizing that their success doesn't diminish your own potential.

Mastering Fear and Greed: The Emotional Drivers of Financial Mistakes

Fear and greed are two of the most powerful emotions that can derail financial decisions.

Chapter 21: The Exodus Blueprint – From Financial Slavery to Sovereignty

This is it. The final page of the final play. You've made it through the maze—dodged the traps, unmasked the puppet masters, seen the blueprint for the beast system for what it is. So now what?

Now, we build the exit.Not an escape into fantasy. But a walkout from the plantation—digital, financial, psychological—that they dressed up as modern life.Because the system wants your soul in chains, but freedom was always your birthright.

I. From Chains to Choices: Acknowledge the GameBefore we can beat the game, we gotta admit it exists.The money system ain't neutral—it was built to benefit the few and bleed the many. Every dollar borrowed, every swipe, every paycheck taxed into thin air while trillionaires roam tax-free—was a brick in a digital prison they hope you never question.But you're here. That means you see it. And if you see it, you can leave it.

Start by shedding the lies:

"Debt is normal." Nah, it's engineered bondage.

"The system cares." It doesn't—it exploits.

"You just need to work harder." You need to work smarter. And freer.

Admitting the truth is the first act of financial revolution.

—-

II. The 5 Pillars of Sovereignty

Here's how we break free—step by practical step.1. Own Your Energy a

Your labor? That's energy. Your attention? That's energy. Your breath, your hustle, your creativity—all the energy they've been harvesting.

Stop giving it away for scraps. Channel it with intention.Build your own income streams.Stop scrolling and start studying.

Use social media to sell, not scroll.

Trade time for equity, not just salary.

Energy, when owned, becomes an empire.

2. Build with Tangible Tools

Digital currency can vanish. Algorithms can erase you. But tangible tools? That's real power.Cash: Keep it alive. Trade with it. Teach it.Land: Own some dirt. Urban, rural, mobile—it doesn't matter. Just own.

Food: Grow it. Store it. Trade it. Learn it.

Skills: Barterable, real-world, income-generating.You don't beat digital feudalism with vibes. beat it with seeds, skills, and sovereignty.3. Circle Over SystemsThey got algorithms. You need ancestors. They got bots. You need brothers and sisters.Build your circle:

Accountability partners who own and build.

Barter networks: plumbers, teachers, creators, cooks.

Local alliances: off-grid thinkers, truth-tellers, prepper crews.

You don't survive the next lockdown alone. You don't beat a system that isolates without community.

4. Educate or Be Enslaved Financial education isn't just smart—it's survival.If you don't understand:

How money works...How debt compounds...How inflation steals...How taxation hides theft...

then you'll always be a pawn.j

Read daily. Teach your kids. Share knowledge like it's food. Because it is.

5. Faith + Fire

You can stack dollars. You can stack gold. But if your spirit ain't fed—you'll break when the test hits.This system ain't just financial—it's spiritual warfare. Babylon with a Wi-Fi signal.So pray. Meditate. Chant. Journal. Build altars.

Chapter 22-The Importantance of credit

In the intricate dance of modern finance, few concepts hold as much sway as credit. Far from being a mere numerical abstract, credit is the bedrock upon which much of our financial lives are built, acting as a powerful determinant of opportunities, costs, and even peace of mind. It's a three-digit number, often encapsulated by the ubiquitous FICO score, but its impact ripples through virtually every major financial decision one makes, from buying a home to securing a job. Understanding credit, its importance, and how to cultivate a healthy credit profile is not just prudent; it's essential for navigating the complexities of economic life and achieving financial goals.

At its most fundamental, credit is a measure of trust. When you apply for a loan, a credit card, or even a rental apartment, the lender or landlord is essentially assessing your creditworthiness – their confidence in your ability and willingness to repay borrowed money or fulfill financial obligations. Your credit score and the underlying credit report serve as a comprehensive report card of your past financial behavior. A strong credit score, typically ranging from the high 600s to the 800s, signals to potential creditors that you are a responsible borrower with a history of timely payments and judicious debt management. This perception of low risk is incredibly valuable, as it directly translates into more favorable terms and access to a wider array of financial products.

The most immediate and tangible benefit of good credit manifests in the realm of borrowing. Whether you're eyeing a mortgage for your dream home, an auto loan for a new car, or a personal loan for a significant expense, your credit score will largely dictate the interest rate you're offered. A higher score can shave substantial percentages off your interest rate, potentially saving you tens of thousands, if not hundreds of thousands, of dollars over the lifetime of a large loan like a mortgage. For example, the difference between a "good" and an "excellent" credit score can mean a difference of a full percentage point or more on a mortgage rate, translating to significantly lower monthly payments and a substantial reduction in the total cost of borrowing. Conversely, a low credit score can either lead to outright loan denials or saddle you with exorbitant interest rates, making major purchases far more expensive and often financially unfeasible. Lenders perceive individuals with poor credit as higher risk, and they compensate for that risk by charging higher interest, essentially making you pay a premium for their uncertainty.

Beyond traditional loans, credit's influence extends to other crucial aspects of life. Renting an apartment, for instance, often involves a credit check by the landlord. A poor credit history can make it challenging to secure housing, as landlords use credit reports to gauge your reliability in meeting financial commitments, including rent payments. In some cases, a low score might require you to pay a larger security deposit or find a co-signer, adding hurdles to an already stressful process. Even utilities like electricity, gas, and water companies may check your credit before approving service, and a less-than-stellar score could necessitate a security deposit.

Moreover, the importance of credit can surprisingly extend into the professional sphere. While employers cannot view your exact credit score, many do conduct modified credit checks as part of their background investigation, especially for positions that involve handling money, sensitive financial data, or significant responsibility. They receive a version of your credit report that omits your date of birth and credit score but reveals aspects of your financial history, such as bankruptcies, late payments, or collections. While laws vary by state regarding the use of credit information for employment decisions, a history of significant financial mismanagement could raise red flags for potential employers, suggesting a lack of responsibility or potential vulnerability to financial pressures. In an increasingly competitive job market, a clean financial slate can subtly give you an edge.

Even your insurance premiums for auto or home insurance can be influenced by your credit-based insurance score. While not identical to your traditional credit score, this specialized score is derived from aspects of your credit report, such as payment history and amounts owed. Insurers use these scores to predict the likelihood of future claims. A higher credit-based insurance score often translates into lower premiums, saving you money on essential coverage. This connection, while perhaps less intuitive, underscores how pervasive credit's reach truly is within the financial ecosystem.

Building and maintaining good credit is a continuous process that hinges on a few core principles. The most critical factor is payment history, which accounts for approximately 35% of your FICO score. Consistently paying all your bills on time – credit cards, loan installments, utilities, and even rent if reported – is paramount. Even a single late payment can significantly ding your score. The amounts owed, or credit utilization, is another major component, making up about 30% of your score. This refers to the amount of credit you're currently using compared to your total available credit. Experts recommend keeping your credit utilization ratio below 30% to avoid appearing overextended. The length of your credit history (around 15%) also plays a role, as a longer history of responsible credit use is generally viewed more favorably. This is why keeping old, well-managed accounts open, even if rarely used, can be beneficial. New credit (around 10%) matters too; opening too many new accounts in a short period can lower your score, as it might signal increased risk. Finally, your credit mix (around 10%), or having a variety of credit types like credit cards, installment loans, and mortgages, can positively impact your score, demonstrating your ability to manage different forms of credit responsibly.

In essence, credit is a powerful financial tool that, when wielded responsibly, unlocks a myriad of opportunities and provides significant financial advantages. It dictates the cost of borrowing, influences housing and insurance prospects, and can even play a subtle role in employment. Cultivating a strong credit profile through diligent financial habits – making timely payments, keeping credit utilization low, and managing a diverse credit portfolio – is not just about a higher number; it's about building a robust financial foundation that provides flexibility, saves money, and paves the way for a more secure and prosperous future. In a world where financial leverage is key, understanding and valuing your credit is an indispensable skill.

Summary

The provided text is a detailed outline and partial draft of "The Money Book," aiming to empower readers with financial literacy and strategies for building wealth and freedom. The content spans twenty chapters, each delving into a critical aspect of personal finance and the broader economic system.

Chapters 1-8 lay the groundwork by challenging conventional wisdom about money, exposing the hidden rules of the financial game, and emphasizing the importance of taking control of one's financial destiny. These chapters likely cover topics such as the history and nature of money, the power of mindset, goal setting, budgeting, understanding debt, and the fundamentals of investing.

Chapters 9-14 delve into more critical and potentially controversial themes, including the rise of digital currencies (CBDCs), social credit systems, the mechanics of debt slavery, the role of AI in finance, and the importance of financial education as a tool for liberation. These chapters suggest a critical perspective on the current financial landscape and advocate for individual empowerment through knowledge and awareness.

Chapters 15-20 focus on actionable strategies for wealth building and protection. Topics covered include the strategic use of debt, building multiple income streams, asset protection, estate planning, navigating the tax system, and cultivating the essential mindset for long-term financial success. These chapters provide practical guidance on how to leverage financial tools and develop the inner resilience needed to achieve financial freedom.

Overall, "The Money Book" appears to be a comprehensive guide that combines financial education with a critical analysis of the current economic system. It encourages readers to become active participants in their financial lives, to understand the hidden forces at play, and to adopt strategies for building wealth, protecting their assets, and ultimately achieving greater financial independence. The tone suggests a direct, no-nonsense approach aimed at "waking up" readers to the realities of the financial world and empowering them to take control.

Did you love *The Digital Trap*? Then you should read *Blood in the Kudzu The Dixie Mafia*[1] by Jm Alexander!

[2]

The South has always been a land of contradictions — sweet tea and bitter truths, Sunday sermons and Saturday night sins. In Blood in the Kudzu, those contradictions take center stage in a chilling account of the Dixie Mafia, one of America's most ruthless and least understood criminal empires.

Born in the poverty-stricken hollows of Mississippi, the Dixie Mafia wasn't a traditional crime family but a sprawling network of misfits, hustlers, and outlaws bound together by a code of loyalty, silence, and fear. They ran whiskey and numbers, trafficked drugs, and left a trail of bodies buried beneath the vines of kudzu that crept over the Southern landscape.From the dirt roads of Yazoo and the gambling

1. https://books2read.com/u/m2ArWR

2. https://books2read.com/u/m2ArWR

dens of Biloxi to the blood-soaked feuds with lawmen like Sheriff Buford Pusser, Blood in the Kudzu traces the rise and fall of men who built power in the shadows. It unpacks their violent methods, their entanglements with politics and police, and the chilling reign of Kirksey Nix — the kingpin who turned prison walls into a command center for extortion and murder.

But this is more than just a true-crime story. It's a portrait of the South itself — a place where injustice fueled rebellion, where corruption and poverty created fertile ground for organized crime, and where every act of defiance left another stain on the land.

Told in a raw, unvarnished voice, Blood in the Kudzu is both memoir and history — a journey through the dark heart of a brotherhood that lived by its own laws, and died by them. For readers of Southern noir, true crime, and outlaw history, this book exposes how the Dixie Mafia grew like the

Also by Jm Alexander

Saturdays in the South

Saturdays in the South The Ole Miss Legacy
Saturday's in the South Hotty Toddy

Standalone

Crossroad Blues
Echos and legends: Introduction to the Harmonica
Controlled Chaos
Flat Earth The ultimate cover up
Blueprint for Deception
Behind the Curtain Hollywood Exposed
AI Apocalypse Rise of the Digital Antichrist
Fabricating Reality
Beyond the Scroll
Revelation Beyond the Pale Horse
The Freedom Lie
The Digital Trap
Erased Histories
The Street Sermon:: Breaking Chains to Change
The Unapologetic Street Sermon A Book on Fred Hampton
Blood in the Kudzu The Dixie Mafia
The 9/11 Conspiracy Theories: A Deep Dive

The Chain Lady Confessions of the Witch of Yazoo
Still I Rise
The Crooked Heart of Ritual
HWY 61 Ghost of the Delta
The Pimp The Prophet and The Limp
Blood Debt
Smoke in the Grove
The Triple Tax
The Acid Test
Hidden God and the Stubborn Dead
Whisper's on the Bayou

About the Author

J.M. Alexander is a truth seeker, storyteller, and founder of Yellaboy Productions, specializing in content creation and literary works that challenge mainstream narratives. With a deep passion for uncovering hidden truths, Alexander explores government cover-ups, historical conspiracies, and the unseen forces shaping society. His works, including Controlled Chaos: Manson and the CIA and Shadow of Deceit: The 9/11 Cover-Up, blend investigative research with compelling storytelling, pushing readers to question everything.

A Mississippi native and lifelong blues enthusiast, Alexander finds inspiration in music, philosophy, and the mysteries of the past. His personal experiences with loss, eerie encounters, and the pursuit of knowledge fuel his writing, making each work a thought-provoking journey. When he's not writing, he's lost in the sounds of Otis Redding or digging into the next great mystery waiting to be unraveled.

About the Publisher

Yellaboy Ink is a truth-seeking platform dedicated to liberating minds through empowering content. We produce diverse works—from compelling publications to multimedia projects—all designed to ignite consciousness and fuel the movement. We are committed to unearthing truth and disseminating knowledge to inspire and empower all who seek it.

Read more at https://jmauthor-gnvcjxvb.manus.space/.

www.ingramcontent.com/pod-product-compliance
Lightning Source LLC
LaVergne TN
LVHW022051200926
848481LV00003B/859
* 9 7 9 8 2 3 1 1 1 7 5 4 3 *